Reclaiming the Gospel of Peace

Challenging the Epidemic of Gun Violence

EDITED BY SHARON ELY PEARSON
Foreword by Mark Beckwith

Morehouse Publishing
NEW YORK

Unless otherwise noted, the Scripture quotations contained herein are from the New Revised Standard Version Bible, copyright © 1989 by the Division of Christian Education of the National Council of Churches of Christ in the U.S.A. Used by permission. All rights reserved.

Morehouse Publishing, 19 East 34th Street, New York, NY 10016
Morehouse Publishing is an imprint of Church Publishing Incorporated.

www.churchpublishing.org

Cover art: *Your Hand in Mine* by Roger Hutchison © 2014
Cover design by Laurie Klein Westhafer
Typeset by Denise Hoff

Library of Congress Cataloging-in-Publication Data
    Reclaiming the gospel of peace : challenging the epidemic of gun violence / Sharon Ely Pearson, editor.
        pages cm
    Includes bibliographical references.
    ISBN 978-0-8192-3202-1 (pbk.)—ISBN 978-0-8192-3203-8 (ebook)
1. Violence—Religious aspects—Episcopal Church.   2. Gun control—United States.   3. Firearms and crime—United States.
4. Violence—Prevention.   5. Peace—Religious aspects—Episcopal Church.   I. Pearson, Sharon Ely, editor.
    BT736.15.R43 2015
    261.8'3315—dc23

                                                                2014037712

Printed in the United States of America

Contents

Part III: *Reclaim: The Response*

Part IV: *Pray: The Work*

Part V: *Engage: The Next Steps*

Foreword

Mark M. Beckwith

In late November 2012, four Episcopal Church bishops, disturbed by the escalating level of gun violence in our cities, agreed to begin conversations with one another in order to figure out how best to bring our faith and resources to bear on a scourge that was reaching epidemic proportions. Two weeks later, the massacre at Sandy Hook Elementary School in Newtown, Connecticut, took place, and immediately the concern about gun violence moved from being a threat contained within urban areas to an issue that gripped the whole country. Other bishops wanted to join the conversation. Our first conference call, held just after Christmas in 2012, included more than a dozen bishops. We prayed, we offered support for one another, we reached out to colleagues, we secured staff help—and we began to plan.

We organized an afternoon symposium at our House of Bishops meeting in March 2013. Vincent Demarco, leader of Faiths United to Prevent Gun Violence and an adjunct professor at Johns Hopkins University in Baltimore, set the context of the gun violence issue in the country. Four bishops—from Connecticut, Chicago, Washington, DC, and Oklahoma—shared how gun violence has affected their faith and their respective dioceses, and how it deepened their commitment to reduce gun violence. (Parts of Oklahoma Bishop Ed Konieczny's presentation are contained in this volume.) The bishops of Connecticut and Washington organized a "Stations of the Cross" procession on Monday of Holy Week 2013, and more than five hundred Episcopalians from across the country (including seventeen bishops) marched through our nation's capital in the snow and rain to make visible the connection between the biblical story of Jesus's death and the story of an average of thirty thousand deaths every year in the United States due to gun violence.

In April 2013 we joined in the lobbying effort to convince key members of the U.S. Senate to pass the Manchin-Toomey bill, which required expanded background checks for gun purchasers. (The resulting vote was just short of a filibuster-proof majority.) That same month several bishops joined with other committed

Episcopal leaders from across the country to design a conference in Oklahoma City to be held in April 2014—"Reclaiming the
Gospel of Peace," many of the presentations from which are contained in this book. We developed a Facebook page, "Episcopalians
Against Gun Violence," and a website, www.bishopsagainstgunvio-
lence.org.

We have written op-eds for our local papers. We began to
develop local networks with other religious leaders. We have continued to build relationships with local politicians, police departments, and other entities committed to reducing gun violence.
We have supported public religious witnesses against gun violence,
notably "Cross Walk" in Chicago and a Good Friday Stations of
the Cross at gun violence sites in Jersey City, New Jersey. We are
encouraging national participation in "Gun Violence Prevention
Sabbath Weekend" on March 20–22, 2015 (the Fourth Sunday in
Lent). We continue to design public worship and witness opportunities, including an outdoor witness to be held at General Convention
in Salt Lake City, Utah, in July 2015.

As our network of bishops has grown, so have the partnerships with other entities within the Episcopal Church, each in its
own way committed to reducing gun violence. I want to thank
Sharon Ely Pearson of Church Publishing Incorporated for her initiative and wisdom in bringing so much important written material
together—from so many different corners of the Episcopal Church,
each reflecting a deepening commitment to reducing gun violence.

From the beginning of our conversations, we have pledged to
provide spiritual and political space for different voices and viewpoints to be expressed and heard. The fifty-two active and retired
bishops of Bishops United Against Gun Violence (as of September
1, 2014) come from across the country, some representing dioceses
that are deeply immersed in gun culture, and others that are largely
resistant to it. Our agenda is to be grounded in the gospel, and to
move forward in a commitment to reducing gun violence—and to
do it together. To that end, we have attempted to reframe the gun
violence conversation from a debate about constitutional rights to
an issue of public health; from the polarizing discourse of gun control to a conversation about gun safety; from the rights of gun users
to a closer scrutiny of gun manufacturers and gun sellers. And to
advocate more intentionally for appropriate background checks—
which polls indicate an overwhelming majority of Americans support, including a sizable majority of gun owners.

We have seen only too often how gun violence tears apart the
fabric of a community. Gun violence is the ultimate act of human

separation: if gun violence doesn't literally separate life from death, gun violence separates people into silos of fear.

There is an urgency for religious communities to step into this vortex of violence and fear. As gun violence creates separation, by definition religion has the capacity to bring people into community. The Latin root of the word "religion"—*religio*—means to bind together. Religion has the capacity, indeed its very purpose, is to create and support community.

The community binding capacity of the Episcopal Church is enormous. When joined with other religious traditions—both within the Christian family and beyond—the capacity to bind broken communities and lives is even greater, and the community fabric can become even stronger. And when we join with mayors (Mayors Against Illegal Guns) and mothers (Moms Demanding Action) who are also deeply committed to reducing gun violence, a powerful and effective witness can be mobilized.

There is a lot of work to do. The challenge can seem overwhelming because, as we know, the forces of resistance are organized and well-funded. As we consider the daunting task ahead, of prayer, advocacy, reflection, and public witness, I invite us to draw on my favorite definition of hope, offered by Jim Wallis, Christian author and witness for social justice: "Hope is believing in spite of the evidence, and then watching the evidence change."

The commitment to reduce gun violence is growing. The partnerships are developing. And as the witness gains momentum, we are seeing the evidence change.

The Rt. Rev. Mark M. Beckwith
Bishop of Newark
Co-convenor, Bishops United Against Gun Violence
The Feast of St. Francis, 2014

Introduction

Sharon Ely Pearson

Thus says the LORD:
A voice is heard in Ramah,
lamentation and bitter weeping.
Rachel is weeping for her children;
she refuses to be comforted for her children,
because they are no more. (Jeremiah 31:15–17)

Using the most recent CDC estimates for yearly deaths by guns in the United States, it is likely that as of August 18, 2014, roughly 58,052 people have died from guns in the United States since the Newtown shootings. If one were to compare that number to the number of deaths *reported in the news* (via the Slate.com partnership with @GunDeaths that has been tracking statistics), the data shows how the story of gun violence in America actually is undertold. On December 14, 2012, Bishop Mariann Edgar Budde of the Diocese of Washington joined with the Very Reverend Gary Hall, dean of Washington National Cathedral, "calling on our national leaders to enact more effective gun control measures. We know from experience that such calls go unheeded. But what if this time you and I took up this issue and wouldn't put it down until something was done? . . . Today we grieve, but soon we act."[1]

The following Sunday, Dean Hall spoke out against gun violence in a sermon that captured the feelings of many Christians as he called upon our country to embrace stricter gun control measures. His statement, "I believe the gun lobby is no match for the cross lobby" became a call to action. "As followers of Jesus, we have the moral obligation to stand for and with the victims of gun violence and to work to end it. The massacre of these twenty-eight people in Connecticut is, for me at least, the last straw. And I believe it is for you. Enough is enough. The Christian community—indeed the entire American faith community—can no longer tolerate this

---

1   A statement released on December 14, 2012, from the Episcopal Diocese of Washington following the shootings at Sandy Hook Elementary School in Newtown, Connecticut.

persistent and escalating gun violence directed against our people. Enough is enough."[2]

Violence in our communities continues to invade our neighborhoods in cities and towns across America. Debates on gun control, legislation, the Second Amendment, and politics continue to divide us instead of drawing us together to make positive change. In April 2014, over two hundred Episcopalians and friends gathered in Oklahoma City for two days to stand and learn with one another how we as the Episcopal Church, corporately and individually, can stand up in unity as violence continues to permeate our society. In the wake of very recent events—the shooting of children at Sandy Hook Elementary School in Newtown, Connecticut, and moviegoers in a theatre in Arvada, Colorado—attendees gathered to pray, listen to presentations, participate in workshops, and exchange ideas and network as a means to begin to work to reclaim the Gospel of Peace in a world that seems out of control. The event concluded with a Eucharist and dinner following a visit to the Oklahoma City National Memorial, the site of the Alfred P. Murrah Federal Building bombing on April 19, 1995, where 168 souls, including 19 children, were lost.

This book is one of those responses. Months have gone by since that April gathering, but violence in our communities continues to proliferate, especially gun violence. While a microcosm of our church met in Oklahoma City, the work that was shared in the presentations and resources (plus others) are within these pages, offered to the wider church—individuals, congregations, and dioceses—to begin to act out in nonviolent ways, to stand for Jesus's gospel of justice, reconciliation, and peace.

I was not able to attend the event, but followed the proceedings through social media, wondering, "What can I do? How can these remarkable words and actions be more accessible to others?" Thus I challenged myself and invited all those who have contributed to this book to make this a reality. My hope is that this can be a resource for the church in which we can teach our children that nonviolence is possible, that we can have a voice in the public arena to speak against violence in our communities, and that by virtue of our baptism we are extolled to proclaim the Gospel of Peace in our words as well as our actions.

Each chapter ends with several reflection questions that can be used individually or in a small group. The book concludes with an Action Guide and list of references and resources so that

---

2   "The Cross Lobby" *Cathedral Age* Easter 2013, 14–17

congregations can begin the process of engaging in the conversation of reclaiming the Gospel of Peace as a faith community in prayerful, respectful, and open ways.

I am grateful to those who accepted my invitation of adding their words to this resource; everyone I approached to contribute to this book said yes. Each essay, resource, and painting was given gratis so that the importance of this work and mission continues. May their thoughts, images, and prayers gathered here provide inspiration and the impetus for each of us to leave our comfort zone and proclaim the Good News of Christ's redeeming love in our homes, churches, cities, and nation. Let us become a Cross Lobby in the truest sense.

Sharon Ely Pearson, editor
Church Publishing Incorporated
The Feast of St. Francis, 2014

PART I

PROCLAIM: THE GOSPEL

"Palestrina Pietà" attributed to Michelangelo Buonarroti (c.1555), now located in the Academy of Fine Arts, Florence, Italy. Photo ©2014 John F. Pearson. Used with permission.

Choose Vulnerability

Caitlin Celella

As an ice hockey player, vulnerability has never been something I prize. Being weak, giving my opponents the opportunity to hurt me, or worse, to let them score on our goalie, is the sure pathway to losing games and never seeing the playoffs. I grew up a fierce tomboy, and being vulnerable meant never getting chosen for a kickball team or failing to outrun the boys, neither of which ever seemed like good options to me. I prided myself on having a tough outer shell and a softer center that only a few could reach.

Surprisingly, the past year and a half has brought many experiences that have shown me the value of becoming vulnerable. God has been showing me, and I have been slow to notice, that I can be strong, but still know when to let others in.

Two summers ago, Bishop Jim Curry invited me to help plan an Episcopal conference on gun violence. I booked my train tickets immediately. Arriving in Baltimore in April last year [2013], with very scant information on what we were there to do, I took a taxi across the city to the cathedral where I ate dinner with the rest of the planning team—a group of twenty bishops, priests, deacons, and some laypeople. We had representations from both coasts and everywhere in between, including the Dioceses of South Dakota, Oklahoma, Colorado, Wyoming, and West Texas.

The meeting opened with norms such as respecting peoples' privacy and ideas, and the ability to call for silent prayer at whim. Bishop Eugene Sutton of Maryland led most of that first night's meeting. He is a tall, formidable man with a low, booming voice, standing at least three feet taller than the wooden podium he was gripping with his large hands. He spoke of listening as wearing another's skin for a time in order to truly try on that person's ideas and opinions. Just as I pondered that definition of listening, it was revealed that this conference was going to tackle the wider problem of violence, not just gun violence. Those from the East and West Coasts were visibly unhappy, as those from the middle of the country seemed like they wanted to escape to their hotel rooms. I was stunned and saddened that simply being Episcopalian was not enough to unite us.

However, Bishop Eugene seemed prepared for this as he refocused us. "Next on the agenda we are going to introduce ourselves. I want each of you to stand up, say your name and your diocese, and what brings you here to the planning session."

For the next hour, everyone in the room sat rapt, listening as individuals stood up to give not only their name, but also their story. One bishop told of his brother's suicide by a firearm many years ago. Some spoke of domestic violence or losing a parishioner to a drive-by shooting. A deacon from Wyoming talked about his state having the highest suicide rate. My introduction went like this: "My name is Caitlin Celella, I'm a lay member of St. Peter's Church in Cheshire, Connecticut, and I'm an English as a Second Language teacher in an inner city. Recently I discovered a student of mine, a kindergartener, sitting outside the principal's office for bringing a toy handgun to school. When I asked him why he brought it, he simply said, 'Because I love it and I don't want to leave it at home all alone.' I am also here because my good friend, fellow camper and camp counselor, Becca Payne, was shot and killed in her Boston apartment a couple years ago. That night, Becca's mother dreamt of her only child, giggling and running down the hallway of their home, only to wake up to the horrible phone call from the Boston Police Department. Someone had busted into her apartment, mistook her for someone else, and ended her life much too early."

As everyone shared their stories, tissues were distributed, and the room seemed to grow smaller. We now knew why we were there to plan this event—every single one of us has a story of violence that we carry with us and that has changed us. On day 2 of planning, a vital question was posed: How can we get

Episcopalians to engage in a conversation about violence? We knew the answer—telling our stories. We had experienced this as a sure way to become vulnerable, to allow everyone listening to wear our skin for a short time, for us to become so human and immediately relatable and accessible to those around us.

That night in Baltimore, I learned the value of telling stories as a way to connect with others, to open honest dialogue, and to pave a path for others to share. To tell your story is to share a piece of yourself, who you are, what has formed you as a person, what makes you tick, and what makes you joyful.

The second of my recent formative experiences occurred at the event we planned, which we titled "Reclaiming the Gospel of Peace: An Episcopal Gathering to Challenge the Epidemic of Violence." My friends all wanted to know, "Why are you flying to Oklahoma City?" The planning team had chosen Oklahoma City very carefully. Our goal was to get everyone to the table—liberals, conservatives, Southerners, Northerners, the old, the young, gun owners and those who don't own guns, and everyone in between—to have an honest conversation about the violence we see daily and what we should be doing about it. Oklahoma City was chosen with the hope of attracting people from all ends of the country to have a conversation the rest of the nation needs to have so desperately, yet cannot seem to have.

The event was held for three days just before Easter 2014 and gathered 220 Episcopalians, including thirty-four bishops, Presiding Bishop Katharine Jefferts-Schori, and the Archbishop of Canterbury Justin Welby. Indeed, there were people from all ends of the country. We had accomplished our first goal of attracting lots of diverse people holding diverse views. Morning worship, Compline, and many shared meals added to our sense of unity and provided time to share our stories and ideas. Most importantly, people came prepared to have an honest discussion about violence! We asked, "What is the cause of the immense and varied violence we see? What violence am I responsible for? What should I be doing?" I was happily surprised that we were able to approach these questions honestly and with the understanding that we are all God's children. I am a twenty-six-year-old woman from the middle of Connecticut, you are a seventy-two-year-old man from West Texas, and upon our meeting we have a familial love that comes from both being children of God. As I greet you, I know there's an aspect of God that I can only see in you. Let's share our stories, our concerns, and what solutions have been effective in our states.

Just as the planning team had discovered in Baltimore, telling our personal stories of violence brought us to see each other as individuals and as equals. Inviting conference participants to share their stories allowed us to begin down the long road of listening to those we had been simply labeling and pigeon-holing, placing in large groups to ignore or yell at from our own corner. Stories shared over drinks or meals or during breaks in the schedule allowed us to connect on a deeper level. The older priest sitting on my left was no longer just a guy from Southern California, as his nametag read; he was now someone who had experienced the abrupt loss of a teenager in his youth group who had committed suicide. During the conference, telling our personal stories of loss, triumph, and even effective actions from our states allowed us to leave labels behind and focus on the important issues at hand.

On the last day of the conference, we took a field trip to the Oklahoma City National Memorial and Museum. We trod somberly through the descriptions of that fateful day almost twenty years ago. From video footage taken by a helicopter mere minutes after the bomb detonated, to rubble dotted with small children's sneakers and office telephones, the museum ended with a stirring "Hall of Honor" with photographs and identifying keepsakes of all 168 victims. This is a memorial of what extreme violence humans are capable of rendering.

We heard a presentation by a survivor of the Oklahoma City bombing, Melissa McLawhorn Houston, who had been working as a lawyer next to the fated Alfred P. Murrah Federal Building. She spoke of crawling out from under a tepee of rubble, finally finding a stairway that would take her to the first floor, and being on autopilot as she found her car to drive home. She spoke of her grandfather, a World War II veteran, who recognized that she was "shell-shocked." She spoke of survivor guilt and her feeling that she should not be alive, her questions about why she was left to live. She went on to work with a group in Washington, DC, to craft some of the nation's first antiterrorism legislation. Melissa said, "One of the biggest ingredients that we see in terrorists is a lack of hope. If you don't have your own sense of hopefulness for your own life, that's where a lot of that starts from."

I thought about how painful it must be for this brave woman to share her story of violence over and over again. She was volunteering to become vulnerable in order to give people a firsthand account of the bombing and how it changed her life. She spoke of a sense of hope for one's own life, which can be fostered by inviting someone in, including them in a group or community, showing them they are worthwhile and loved. Being accepted into a community, valued as a person with stories to share, can provide a true ray of hope in someone's otherwise dark, lonely, and hopeless life.

The teens in this parish's [St. Peter's] Journey to Adulthood (J2A) youth group know this already. I once asked them on a sleepy Sunday morning, "How can we become people who sacrifice for others?" One teen immediately replied, "By talking to people, getting to know them." The group agreed that talking with someone is sometimes avoided because of how the person looks or rumors we've heard about them. When asked what they need to be able to get students in their schools talking to each other, they decided they need the time, safe space, and chocolate (some kind of tasty food to gather around).

Not long after that J2A meeting, the "Lenten Friends and Faith at Home" groups began. My husband, Andy, and I were blessed to have the chance to offer our small home to an expanded version of the young adults' Theology on Tap group. For this Lenten series, our group featured those as seasoned as seventy-eight-years-old and as young as twenty-five. The expert prompts of short video clips, Scripture, and questions led to all of us taking risks—sharing our own stories of triumph and growth as well as loss, violence, and struggling to forgive. I saw that the J2A group was entirely correct—given the time, safe space, and chocolate (or a beverage of one's choice), a group could easily engage with each other and get to know each other on a much deeper level. I found myself choosing to tell personal stories as others listened attentively, also willing to take on others' pain as I wore their skin for a short time. I had no problem becoming vulnerable in front of this group, and others chose to do the same. Personal growth occurred through listening to others' stories and wrestling with questions like, "Is every action forgivable?" or working together to brainstorm ways to capture the feeling of gratefulness every morning. Again, I had found that our stories encouraged others to share, to be honest with ourselves, and to forget age or which worship service we attend. We grew in our love for each other and for our model of love, Christ.

The reading from 1 Peter (3:13–22) said, "In your hearts revere Christ as Lord. Always be prepared to give an answer to everyone who asks you to give the reason for the hope that you have."[3] This hope is the love of Christ that the world needs to know about and

---

3   Scripture taken from the HOLY BIBLE, TODAY'S NEW INTERNATIONAL VERSION ® TNIV ® Copyright © 2001, 2005 by Biblica www.biblica.com. All rights reserved worldwide.

that we need to share with others. This is also my hope; that we love each other enough to come together as a nation, as a united people, to have an honest discussion about how to protect our citizens—our children—from violence. As I experienced with the planning team, the "Reclaiming the Gospel of Peace" conference, the J2A youth group, and the Friends and Faith at Home Lenten series, this hope of Christ involves choosing to become vulnerable, to share our stories, to set aside the labels of Democrat and Republican and Independent, Northerner and Southerner, male and female, and to get to the bottom of what makes us human and what makes us followers of Christ—our love for one another and our willingness to share that love with everyone—especially if we need to choose vulnerability to get there.

I'm willing to choose vulnerability—are you?

Ms. Caitlin Celella lives in Connecticut with her beloved husband and giant dog. A lifelong member of St. Peter's Episcopal Church in Cheshire, Connecticut, Caitlin sings in the choir, leads youth group, and times everyone's sermons. She is chair of the ESL department at Holy Apostles College and Seminary in Cromwell, Connecticut. She preached this sermon on May 25, 2014 (Sixth Sunday of Easter, Year A), soon after her return from the conference in Oklahoma City.

For Reflection
1. Where is your story in this story?
2. Where do you see God?
3. What causes you to pause and rethink your previous assumptions?
4. What cries out to you?
5. What calls to you?

Go Deeper
1. When have you allowed yourself to be vulnerable?
2. How has your life been touched by violence? What story could you share?
3. What is your hope for the future?

Why Are We Here?

Edward J. Konieczny

On December 14, 2012, a young twenty-year-old man entered Sandy Hook Elementary School in Newtown, Connecticut, and fatally shot twenty children and six adult staff members. Before driving to the school, the young man shot and killed his mother in their home; and then as first responders arrived at the school, he shot and killed himself. The incident at Sandy Hook Elementary School was not the first of these kinds of incidents in our society; and has not been the last.

In 1966, a former Marine killed sixteen people and wounded thirty others at the University of Texas.

In 1973, a twenty-three-year-old man killed nine people at a Howard Johnson's motel.

In 1986, a part-time mail carrier killed fourteen postal workers in a post office, here, in Edmond, Oklahoma, leading to the often and unfortunately used phrase: "Going Postal."

In 1999, two young men, eighteen and seventeen years old killed twelve students and a teacher at Columbine High School in Colorado.

In 2007, a twenty-three-year old student killed thirty-two people at Virginia Tech University.

In 2012, a twenty-four-year-old man killed twelve and wounded fifty-eight others in a movie theatre in Aurora, Colorado.

In 2013, a civilian contractor fatally shot twelve and wounded three others inside the Washington Navy Ship Yard.

And just this morning, a student moved through a school in Murrysvania, Pennsylvania, stabbing and slashing more than twenty others before being taken into custody.

These are just a few; in the last thirty years there have been more than sixty mass killings in the United States; and this doesn't even begin to take into account the single acts of violence resulting in loss of life, wounding, and maiming that occurs every day in our cities, towns, and communities across this country.

By any definition of the word, the frequency of violent acts in our society is of epidemic proportion. With what always seems to be predictable regularity, what follows these incidents are the speculations of motive, the armchair psychological profiling, the ideological positioning, the political rhetoric, and the finger-pointing, trying to cast blame on someone or something. And sadly, after a few weeks, the shock and devastation dissipates from those not directly affected; our attentions are drawn elsewhere; politicians move on to the next political debate; and we are left wondering why and how and won't anything ever be done . . .

Doing something is why we are here . . .

For years people have cried out for the authorities or politicians to enforce existing laws and pass new ones. For years people have pointed the finger at this or that as the cause for the violence in our society. For years the polarizing voices of the extremes have dominated the conversation, entrenched in their idealistic positions and agendas, and stifled any attempt for a reasoned, commonsense conversation and approach to challenging the increased incident of violence around us.

We are not here to cast blame, or to produce some statement or resolution calling on others to act, or to be drowned out by those who want to intimidate. We are here to have a new conversation: a conversation that says we are not willing to accept that violence is a natural part of society; a conversation that acknowledges we live in relationship, and that we are all responsible for how we treat one another; a conversation that talks about how each of us can make a difference, about how each one of us can change the trajectory of violence in our world; a conversation that recognizes and honors the diversity of voices and perspectives and passions.

So how is it that I am standing before you today? I represent one of those diverse voices. So let me share a little of my story . . .

It was a little over a year ago when I received a call from the bishop of Connecticut, Ian Douglas. Ian asked if I would be willing to participate in a panel discussion at our spring House of Bishops' Meeting to reflect about gun control and violence in our society following the horrific incident at Sandy Hook. In all honesty I was surprised by Ian's call. I told Ian that I didn't think my perspective would be welcome as part of the discussion. I shared with him that I was a former cop, having served for nearly twenty years in Southern California; I support the Constitutional Right to Bear Arms; I have a CCW Permit, and on occasion have been accused of being a "gun-toting bishop." I suggested that he might want to reconsider his invitation. After all, my voice was not exactly in the mainstream of political correctness.

Ian paused and said, "Your voice and perspective is absolutely needed in this conversation." He said, "If we are ever going to be able to change the incidence of violence in our society, then all voices need to be heard. We need to do something other than entrench ourselves in ideological positions." So, with a little persuasion, encouragement, and arm-twisting, Ian convinced me that my voice, my experience, might add something to the conversation.

As I prepared my remarks for that meeting, I became very aware of a tension, an internal struggle that was challenging me to get past my long-held party line perspectives and dig deeper into what I was truly feeling. As a former police officer, I can say that we work hard at meticulously building walls and putting up protective barriers to protect ourselves from emotions and feelings. The myth is that having emotions and feelings is a detriment to doing the job. What I discovered while preparing those remarks was that maybe I did have some emotions and feelings. That maybe over the years some cracks had developed in those walls.

At that House meeting I started my remarks with what I had said to Ian, "You should know I am a gun owner; I have a CCW [carry concealed weapon] Permit; and I occasionally carry a gun when traveling throughout the state of Oklahoma."

And then I went on to share some of my experience.

In 1979, one of my best friends and fellow police officer, Don Reed, agreed to swap shifts with me so I could have a weekend off to of all things, play in a police softball tournament. During that shift, Don responded to a call at a local bar where he confronted a man who was later determined to be a convicted felon, recently released from prison, and who had recently purchased several guns. As Don was escorting the man out of the bar with other officers, the man took a semiautomatic handgun out from under his coat and shot Don several times in the chest. Don died at the scene. The suspect eluded police for several days, but was eventually captured, convicted, and sentenced to life in prison.

In 1982, as the lead investigator working on a crime task force, I was assigned the case of a prison escapee who was a serial rapist. The suspect was reportedly responsible for more than twenty brutal rapes, usually pistol-whipping his victims. Early on a Sunday morning I received a tip from an informant that the suspect was heading to the Santa Ana area of Orange County. Staking out the area with other officers, the suspect appeared in the stolen vehicle of his most recent victim. A pursuit ensued with the suspect losing control of his vehicle and crashing into a telephone pole. The suspect exited his vehicle and in an exchange of gunfire, he was shot and killed.

In 1991, a couple of days before I was to leave the police department for seminary, I was dispatched to a "check the welfare" call. Family members had been unable to contact a brother who had been suffering from depression. Getting no response from knocks on the door, we checked and found the front door of the residence unlocked. Upon opening the door, the man appeared directly in front of me with a rifle pointed at my head. The man pulled the trigger but the gun misfired. The man was subsequently arrested and taken for a psychiatric evaluation. It was later determined he had been suffering from mental illness for years, yet was still able to purchase a gun.

As I made these remarks to my fellow bishops, a flood of emotions began to well up within me and I came face-to-face with my reality: I live everyday knowing that I share responsibility for taking a human life, and but for the grace of God I would not be standing here today.

These incidents, the tragedy at Sandy Hook, and all the other incidents of violence, hatred, intolerance, and death seem to collide within me, I am left wondering how we got here. What have we as a people done or failed to do that causes someone to think that their only option is to act out in some violent way?

And then there was this question: "What are you going to do about it?"

For years these tragedies have been occurring, and while there may have been momentary calls for changes in laws or political rhetoric, what seems to be happening is that our world, our society, our communities are willing to accept this as the new norm. That we should all just get used to it because it is going to happen again and again and again.

[After that House Meeting, I decided] I am not willing to accept that. . . . I refuse to feel powerless; that I cannot make a difference or have an influence. I refuse because I know better. I refuse because I have seen lives changed and relationships restored. I have seen youth who have felt outcast and lonely and unworthy come to know that they are beloved children of God, cared for, and respected, and valued. I have seen teenagers and young adults caught in the vicious cycles of life given a new sense of purpose. I have seen adults incarcerated for the mistakes they made renewed, reconciled, and restored. I have seen how the faces of the homeless light up when they are treated with dignity and respect.

I am not willing to accept that we are destined to suffer the tragedies that have plagued our society. Instead I am convinced that we can change judgmental attitudes, intolerant behaviors, and the violence in our society.

Each and every one of us has the power to make a difference. We do it by proclaiming by word and example the Good News of God in Christ. We do it by seeking and serving Christ in all people, loving our neighbors as ourselves. We do it by striving for justice and peace among all people and respecting the dignity of every human being.

These words may sound familiar. They should. They are the foundations of our Baptismal Covenant. You see, we don't have to figure out what to do; we just have to do that which we have already promised. Each and every one of us here has the ability to make a difference: one person, one life at a time. And the time is now.

We didn't get to where we are today overnight, or in a year or even a decade. It has taken generations. There are those who would say we're not going to change it overnight or in a year or in a decade. It is going to take generations. But there was a Jewish philosopher who once said in the first century, "If not now, when? And if not me, who?"[4]

It is time that we as people of faith stand up and proclaim something new to this hurt and broken and violent world. It is time that we as people of faith reclaim that which we have been

---

4   Attributed to Hillel the Elder (c. 110 BCE–10 CE).

blessed and given. It is time that we begin a new conversation and that our voices instill a new mantra in the world: That all are created in the image of God; that all are children of God, and all deserve respect and dignity.

My hope is that this conference might be a model, an example to others of how differing voices, with often very opposite passions, can come together with honesty, charity, and grace for a common purpose. As we go about our time together over these next couple of days, let's keep in our hearts and minds all those who have been victims of violence, especially those who suffered that attack of this morning.

May God bless our time together, and may God make us instruments of His peace!

The Right Reverend Dr. Edward J. Konieczny is the fifth bishop of Oklahoma, consecrated in 2007. From 1975 until 1992, Bishop Ed served as a police officer with the Garden Grove and Anaheim Police Departments. His assignments varied from uniformed patrol to child abuse/sexual assault to vice. He was ordained a deacon and priest in 1994. This was the opening address for the "Reclaiming the Gospel of Peace" conference delivered on April 9, 2014, in Midwest City / Oklahoma City.

For Reflection

1. Where is your story in this story?
2. Where do you see God?
3. What causes you to pause and rethink your previous assumptions?
4. What cries out to you?
5. What calls to you?

Go Deeper

1. Do you feel you can change the trajectory of violence in our world? If so, how? If not, why not?
2. Does a tension lie within you about gun ownership?
3. What is your experience of encounters with police officers?

4. What have we as a people done or failed to do that causes someone to think that their only option is to act out in some violent way?
5. What are you not willing to accept about the state of violence in our communities?

Challenging the Mythology of Violence

Eugene Taylor Sutton

Let us pray.
Come by here, my Lord, come by here.
Come by here, my Lord, come by here.
O Lord, come by here.
Someone's dying Lord, come by here.
Someone's dying Lord, come by here.
Someone's dying Lord, come by here.
O Lord, come by here.
Be present, be present Lord Jesus.

At this gathering, the Episcopal Church aims to model a civil and respectful conversation about violence in general and gun violence in particular—a dialogue that our society has not been able to accomplish. It arises out of a dream that a number of us had of gathering together Episcopalians from across the spectrum of geographical, political, and theological differences to learn from each other, pray with each other, and discern together what the Spirit may be saying to us as church leaders. In order to do this, we need to agree to make this a safe space, a "condemnation-free zone" for the next three days.

It will not help us to prejudge each other here. Do not assume that just because someone owns firearms that she or he is a rightwing, violence-prone, conspiracy theorist who does not want to end gun violence in our cities, towns, and rural places. And, on the other hand, do not assume that just because someone supports legislation to put limits on gun ownership that he or she is a left-wing, un-American, Constitution-tearing snob who wants to take away your private property and who does not himself or herself own firearms. These are all unhelpful conversation starters, and not conducive to the building up of Christian community! So let's leave all prejudgments at the door, agreed?

What this means is that we are here to listen as much as we are here to advocate positions. "Listening is the act of entering the skin of the other and wearing it for a time as if it were our own."[5] It is in this climate of tolerance and respect that we can begin to address a major public health crisis in our country that is increasingly defining our image both here and abroad.

In the United States of America, the world's only remaining superpower and self-proclaimed moral force for good in the world, thirty thousand of its citizens are killed every year by firearms. Another estimated one hundred thousand are shot every year, most of whom will carry permanent injuries, and all of whom will carry emotional scars for the rest of their lives. Just think about these figures; what it means is that every eight to ten years, one million people are shot in this country.

This comes at a tremendous cost to our society: one million emergency room scenes, one million families grieving, one million victims and survivors trying to put broken bodies and wounded souls back together again. The financial costs to our health system, the long-term costs of physical rehabilitation, and the emotional costs to the victims and their families last for decades.

The violence affects us all. Whether it is in the middle-class enclaves of Newtown, Connecticut, on a Native American reservation in the Dakota plains, a school campus in Colorado or Arkansas, an Army base in Texas, or on some forgotten street in Baltimore, Maryland—we are a nation in mourning over the killing of its children. What's going to stop the epidemic of violence in our state, in or country, and in our world? The Christian gospel has proclaimed for thousands of years that there is a cure—but we have lost confidence in our day that that ancient solution will work. For according to the gospel of Jesus Christ, the cure for violence is love.

---

5   David Spangler, *Parent as Mystic, Mystic as Parent* (New York: Riverhead Trade, 2000), 70

Jesus said, "Love your enemies, do good to those who hate you, bless those who curse you, pray for those who abuse you" (Luke 6:27–28).

What? Our violence-ridden culture would have us believe that what Jesus said in the gospel were wonderful words back two thousand years ago, and they may have worked well back there in Galilee, but we live in the real world in a very dangerous twenty-first century. Love your enemies? Love those who want to harm you? No, we must fight our enemies, outwit and outmaneuver our enemies, destroy and kill our enemies before they destroy and kill us.

And yet, Martin Luther King Jr. many years ago had this to say about these words of Jesus: "Jesus has become the practical realist. . . . Far from being the pious injunction of a utopian dreamer, the command [to love others] is an absolute necessity for the survival of our civilization. Yes, it is love that will save our world and our civilization, love even for enemies."[6]

Well, how can it actually work? I remember a story that Gerald May, the Christian psychotherapist and spiritual guide at the Shalem Institute for Spiritual Formation in the Washington area, once recounted: "It was in 1976, and I had just received my first-level belt in the gentle Japanese martial art of Aikido: the practice (do) of the harmony (ai) of the universal energy (ki). A visiting master called me to the front of the room and he asked me to attack him. He stood quietly as I charged at him, then turned his head slightly away. My speed increased as I felt powerfully drawn toward him. Then he bowed his head slightly and looked back at me, and I found myself lying comfortably on the floor. We had not even touched . . .

"He explained that he had aligned himself with my attacking energy, joined it from his own centered stillness, and gently guided it back around me towards the ground. From my perspective, it seemed I had inexplicably decided to lie down and rest."

What was that force, that nonviolent power? Power, in human terms, is the ability and use of force to accomplish one's will over persons or situations. But *dunamis*, the word for "power" which occurs over 120 times in the New Testament, is a creative, dynamic power that is very different from the "power over" aspects of

6   "Loving Your Enemies," sermon, Dexter Avenue Baptist Church, Montgomery, Alabama, November 17, 1957, http://mlk-kpp01.stanford.edu/index.php/encyclopedia/ documentsentry/doc_loving_your_enemies/.

human force or control. *Dunamis* is spiritual power; the power that can only come from God.

As for human, or worldly, power, the United States is unquestionably the most powerful nation in the world. We have unparalleled economic power, so much so that it is said when the US economy sneezes, the rest of the world catches a cold. We have immense technological power that enables American influence and culture to be felt to the farthest reaches of the earth—even into the universe. We have unmatched military power, with capabilities of destroying targets with pinpoint accuracy from hundreds of miles away.

And yet, with all the power that is possible to acquire on this earth, still the United States of America is not able to force the rest of the world to act in accordance with our will, or to further our own national goals wherever and whenever we desire. Despite our massive human power, we frequently find ourselves powerless to get persons or situations or countries under our control. We find that we cannot force others to do what they do not want to do.

So we need to make a distinction between power, on the one hand, and control on the other. To illustrate that difference, I want to tell you about Louise. Several years ago in Mason, Tennessee, an elderly black woman named Louise Degrafinried astounded the nation when she persuaded an escaped convict from a local prison to surrender. He had a gun, and with his gun, he thought he had control. He had surprised Louise's husband, Nathan, outside their modest home and forced himself inside.

But Louise was not afraid of the gun. The short, grandmotherly woman told the convict to put his gun down while she fixed him some breakfast. Now, I don't know if you know anything about the amazing curative powers of a Southern home-cooked breakfast; it's really built around fat. While cooking the meal, Louise spoke of her faith and how a young man such as he should behave, and that with God's help he could turn his life around. Between the breakfast and her words, in no time at all, the young man was on his way back to the Tennessee prison.

The escaped convict had control, the control of the gun. But Louise Degrafinried had power.

There is a fundamental distinction between control and power. It is very important that we see it, both in our personal lives, in our society, and in our theology. God, we say, is "omnipotent"—all-powerful—and that is true, but we must not confuse that power with control. God is all-power, but not all-control. God has plenty of power, but chooses to exercise little control over the world.

The unchecked human need for control arises out of fear: fear of a chaotic and unsafe world. "If only the world were more predictable," we think, "then I would feel better, I would feel safe." It is because of fear that humans tend to theologize a controlling God. Thus we also tend to believe that it is our duty, led by a controlling God, to control others by any of the means of control at our disposal—especially weapons. And there lies the idolatry.

The agenda of God is not to control, but to love. Love always seeks the best for the beloved, even at great cost. "God so loved the world that he gave his only Son . . . [not] to condemn the world [but to save it]" (John 3:16–17).

The power of love to change the world cannot be underestimated. To quote Martin Luther King Jr. again, he called that kind of power "soul force." The great American civil rights leader learned the principles of soul force from his reading of the ethics of Jesus, and from Gandhi's use of the phrase to describe his methods of nonviolent resistance.

In terms of social change, "soul force" is based in the power of an idea: freedom. If our great nation has any real power at all, it is in the abundance of freedom that we enjoy here and our willingness to share this power with the world. It is the only export that we have that has power over others—not money, not bombs, not self-interest, but freedom. Archbishop Desmond Tutu once said, "When a people decide they want to be free, then nothing can stop them."[7] They can even stare down the barrel of a gun—and they will prevail.

This soul force is not only the power to change human lives, but it is the most effective force that is available to humans to change whole societies toward the vision of God for the world. In the book *A Force More Powerful,* written by Peter Ackerman and Jack DuVall (Palgrave Macmillan, 2000), the authors carefully document over fifteen movements of mass social change that have resisted systems of injustice on every continent of the world. They have concluded that the twentieth century should have been known as the century that has demonstrated the triumph of nonviolent action as the most powerful force in the world. This massive and well-documented book reminds us that

- it wasn't physical force that drove the mighty British empire from colonial India in 1947, it was soul force.

---

7   Desmond Tutu, videotaped interview by Steve York for the documentary television series *A Force More Powerful,* Atlanta, Georgia, August 27, 1999.

- it wasn't physical force that successfully resisted the Nazis in Denmark and saved many Jews, it was soul force.
- it wasn't physical force that brought down the dictator General Martinez in El Salvador in 1944.
- it wasn't physical force that brought down segregation in the American South in the 50s and 60s.
- it wasn't physical force that restored democracy to the Philippines in 1986.
- it wasn't physical or violent force that moved Lech Walesa and Solidarity into power in Poland.
- it wasn't physical force that brought down totalitarian regimes in the former USSR and Eastern Europe.
- it wasn't physical force that dismantled apartheid and the racist government in South Africa.

In each case, it was soul force.

If the above representative list seems new or shocking to you, it is because we have done a poor job in this country of teaching any of the principles of nonviolent action as a way of solving conflicts. We don't do it. Many fear that our culture will never do this, because we have become intoxicated with violence as the only effective means to achieve our personal goals and national aspirations. We have worshiped for too long at the altar of the gun to solve our problems. This has led to what can be called "The Mythology of Violence"; namely, the widely held myth that violence works, and that nonviolence is a pipe dream for idealists who do not know how the world really operates.

I want to emphasize here that there is a time-honored tradition in Christianity of sometimes having to resort to a "just war" in certain extraordinary circumstances, and we are very dependent upon our brave men and women in the armed forces who are sometimes called upon to fight and put themselves in harm's way on our behalf. We are grateful for their service and the service of all uniformed people; we pray for them and for our leaders to make wise decisions before sending them into armed conflict. But you do not need to be a pacifist like Jesus, Gandhi, or King in order to learn any of the almost two hundred methods of nonviolent action that have been proven to be effective in removing unjust institutions and governments, and restoring peace and freedom. As Christians, as followers of Christ, we are called upon to teach peace as well as to practice peace, which means we have to continually relearn the ways of peace in a culture that's awash in violence. We must repent, both individually and collectively, for believing that violence and killing will be the answer.

Just this past week I had the privilege of spending some time in Baltimore with the former Archbishop of Canterbury Rowan Williams, who was there to give a lecture. I told him about this conference addressing violence, and I reminded him of some words he said eleven years ago that had a profound effect on me in my thinking about violence. It was early 2003 when our nation was embroiled in an intense debate on whether or not the United States should invade Iraq to address the problem of Saddam Hussein and his supposed weapons of mass destruction. Dr. Williams said at that time,

"If all you have is hammers, then all you see is nails."[8]

His warning was clear. If we put our trust only in guns and bombs to make peace, then we only see solutions that demand the use of guns and bombs.

Perhaps Martin Luther King Jr. can teach us once again how to "live together as [family] or die together as fools." Six months before he was cut down by an assassin's bullet, he said this in a sermon:

> To our most bitter opponents we say: "We shall match your capacity to inflict suffering by our capacity to endure suffering. We shall meet your physical force with soul force. Do to us what you will, and we shall continue to love you. We cannot in all good conscience obey your unjust laws, because non-cooperation with evil is as much a moral obligation as is cooperation with good. Throw us in jail, and we shall still love you. Send your hooded per- petrators of violence into our communities at the mid- night hour and beat us and leave us half dead, and we shall still love you. But be ye assured that we will wear you down by our capacity to love. One day we shall win freedom, but not only for ourselves. We shall so appeal to your heart and conscience that we shall win you in the process, and our victory will be a double victory."

That is the power of love. We need to teach that. That is soul force . . . the way of Jesus.

---

8   BBC Radio 4, "Thought for the Day." December 23, 2012.

The Right Reverend Eugene Taylor Sutton has been bishop of the Episcopal Diocese of Maryland since June 2008. Previously he served as canon pastor of Washington National Cathedral and director of the Cathedral Center for Prayer and Pilgrimage. This was his plenary address given at the "Reclaiming the Gospel of Peace" conference on April 9, 2014, in Oklahoma City.

For Reflection

1. Where is your story in this story?
2. Where do you see God?
3. What causes you to pause and rethink your previous assumptions?
4. What cries out to you?
5. What calls to you?

Go Deeper

1. What does the word "power" mean to you?
2. What kinds of power do you have?
3. When do you feel powerless?
4. What do you have control over?
5. What is your soul force?

Why Gun Violence Is a Religious Problem

Gary R. Hall

December's horrific shootings at Sandy Hook Elementary School in Newtown, Connecticut, came at the end of a year filled with shocking gun deaths. Three were mass shootings, as at the Wisconsin Sikh Temple and the movie theater in Aurora, Colorado. There was the daily drumbeat of gun deaths in urban neighborhoods across America. Something about the Newtown massacre finally prompted many preachers, including me, to address the problem. "Enough," we said, "Was enough."

Those of us who have taken on the gun issue in pulpits have received much response—most of it positive, some of it critical. We are lauded for taking a public stand on an important issue, taken to task for mixing politics and religion. From the beginning of my foray into this matter, I have consistently said that the Church should address it because gun violence is primarily a religious issue. I'd like to use this opportunity to explain what I mean.

Defining Evil

In the early days following the Newtown shootings, I was called on in interviews to respond to a characterization of that event as an example of evil. It happens, however, that I had the opportunity to do some extended thinking about evil as a philosophical and religious problem in the year before I came to the Cathedral: I taught a class to seniors at Cranbrook School, where I was serving as chaplain, called "The Problem with Evil." This was not a class I would have thought up on my own; I took it over from a faculty colleague who had to leave school suddenly because of a family emergency.

One of the things I learned in preparing for that class is that our definition of evil has changed over time, though we have always defined evil as having to do with the suffering of the innocent; we talk about evil differently in the post-twentieth-century world from how we did before. Before the modern (let alone postmodern) era, people tended to think of evil as something with cosmic cause: the innocent suffered because they were possessed by demons, say, or because the larger evil force personified as Satan created chaos. In the age of science, though, our definition of evil has shifted: we now increasingly define "evil" as something caused by human agency: genocide, oppression, sexual abuse.

When the 2011 earthquake struck Washington National Cathedral, nobody characterized that event as an example of evil. When the 2012 shootings at Newtown happened, though, everyone did. Prior to the twentieth century, clergy were routinely called on to explain the meaning of natural calamities. Nowadays we're asked instead to address the disasters made by human beings.

Human Suffering

Whether we think of evil as caused by cosmic or human activity, the problem of innocent human suffering is still a core religious question. Every major religion attempts to explain (or at least respond to) suffering. In our own tradition, the Bible gives us the story of Job and, of course, the example of Jesus.

Job—the exemplary man whose children, possessions, and health are taken from him for no fault of his own—is an example of the premodern sufferer. Jesus—the exemplary man who dies at the hands of what the old Prayer Book called "sinful men"—could be said to be the first example of modern or postmodern suffering. Both are innocent. One suffers at the hand of God, one suffers at the hand of people. Neither deserve what they get. We are left to make sense of their sufferings as best we can.

Christians (as well as Jews and Muslims) have long found the meaning of innocent suffering less in speculation about its cause and more in the response it elicits from us. Think of Jesus's parable of the Good Samaritan, where three people leave a man to die in the road and only one responds by giving him aid. Think of the crucifixion of Jesus himself, which arouses the compassionate response of the men and women who were his companions. Think of the book of Acts, where the earliest Christian community is seen as a sort of underground social service network, bringing aid and comfort to those cast aside by the Roman Empire. The Bible may not speak with one voice about why suffering happens, but it is unanimous in its claim that human suffering demands the active response of faithful people. Jesus was probably more famous in his day as a healer than as a teacher. God's will is that people live whole, free, joyful lives. And God has gathered a community who will work to bring wholeness, freedom, and joy wherever there is sickness, oppression, and pain.

So one way to understand the Church's call to end gun violence in America (or at least greatly reduce it) is to see this call as the natural consequence of our compassionate response to human suffering. We follow One who died at the hands of violence. That One has called us to be agents of love and healing in the world. The only way we can address large-scale questions of love and justice is in the public arena. And when we enter the public arena, we necessarily have to do with the politics.

A Public Church

When people complain that activism to eliminate gun violence is political and that preachers should get back to religion and leave politics to others, I have two responses. One is about the nature of public life. The other is about the nature of public church.

Christians have no warrant to think magically. If we are to be postmodern (and not premodern) in our response to evil, then we will have to agree that, for us in the twenty-first century, the problem of evil is a human problem. Innocent people die because people do bad things. Societies deal with people who do bad things by acting corporately to prevent and punish bad behavior. They act corporately by means of legislative action. Because we live in a republican democracy, our laws are enacted not from above but by means of political organizing. If we want to deal with a public, human problem, then politics are necessarily going to be involved. "Politics" is not a dirty word. It's the way human beings organize their social lives.

For us Christians, the Bible is the source of our teaching on moral and ethical issues. And when we look at the Bible for guidance, we discover what often surprises people who are unfamiliar with the Scriptures. Instead of being preoccupied with the individualistic moral problems that dominate our contemporary thought, the Bible is overwhelmingly concerned with public—not private—morality. The big problems for the Bible's voices (the prophets and Jesus) are social issues: economic justice, relief for widows and orphans, fair treatment of those who live at life's margins. For every admonition about personal behavior, the Bible probably has five exhortations toward social compassion and justice. The pervasive individualism of American culture tends to read the Bible though the lens of its own preoccupations and so to cast morality as primarily a personal or private affair. But morality for the Bible is primarily a public business. For the Scriptures, justice in Israel is a higher priority than personal moral decisions. It's not that the latter are not important; it's just that the former is exponentially more so.

Taking Action

All of which leads me to say that reducing gun violence and taking the necessary political steps to do so are, at their root, profoundly spiritual concerns. As people of faith, we are repeatedly asked to respond to and alleviate the suffering of the innocent. However you define evil—whether it's caused by the devil or by a madman— faithfulness to Jesus and the One he calls his Father demands that we respond in compassion. Because there is nothing we can do to prevent national disasters, when tsunamis and earthquakes happen the best we can do is send aid. Human behavior is responsive to concerted action. When malevolence causes the deaths of children— in schoolrooms and on city streets—we can and must take action both to heal and to stop it. A church that did nothing in the face of innocent suffering wouldn't be worthy of the name.

Although I am the leader of Washington National Cathedral, I do not presume to speak for the Cathedral or its members. But I do try to articulate what I hear God calling us to do. I realize that everyone in our life does not agree with me. Anglicanism is a comprehensive tradition, and people of good will can differ about the best means to address questions of social and personal suffering. The goal, of course, is to eliminate gun violence. The exact mix of the ways we do that—gun legislation, mental health reform, a more critical look at the culture of violence—is open to conversation.

I believe that the goal and the dialogue around it are holy, and that we are acting in the best, deepest traditions of the Gospel when we take up these questions and act on behalf of past, present, and future victims.

"All we like sheep have gone astray. We have turned everyone to his own way. And the Lord has laid on him the iniquity of us all." Isaiah's words are routinely applied to Jesus, and they could be said of the victims of Newtown, Aurora, Columbine, and Virginia Tech too. I ask that you join me by studying, thinking, praying, and acting to stop gun violence in America. How we face into and address the iniquity laid on Jesus and those who die violently will prove the measure of what kind of a church we finally are.

The Very Reverend Gary R. Hall has been the tenth dean of Washington National Cathedral since 2012. He was dean and president of Seabury-Western Theological Seminary in Evanston, Illinois, from 2005–2010 and has served in numerous congregations. This article was first published in the Diocese of Washington's magazine, *Cathedral Age* (Easter 2013): 14–17.

For Reflection

1.   Where is your story in this story?
2.   Where do you see God?
3.   What causes you to pause and rethink your previous assumptions?
4.   What cries out to you?
5.   What calls to you?

Go Deeper

1.   Do you believe gun violence is a religious issue? Why or why not?
2.   What is your definition of "evil"?
3.   "The Bible is unanimous in its claiming that human suffering demands the active response of faithful people." Do you agree? Why? Disagree? Why?
4.   How "public" should the Church be in addressing social concerns?
5.   As a person of faith, how do you respond to and alleviate the suffering of the innocent?

Custody of the Heart

Katharine Jefferts Schori

Love your enemies and pray for those who persecute you. The ability to do that begins with the heart. There's a traditional Irish prayer that goes something like this, "May those who love us love us. And those who don't love us, may God turn their hearts. And if he doesn't turn their hearts, may he turn their ankles so we will know them by their limping."

That is a start, and it's honest—it doesn't hide the complexity of feeling about an enemy. But those who would be perfect, as Jesus charges us, have to keep looking beyond subtle forms of vengeance or branding those we deem unlovable with some obvious sign of their irredeemability—as though we might not have to try so hard to love them. Learning to live without violence is an ongoing struggle.

Violence is anything that seeks to diminish life—especially another person's integrity or dignity or life possibilities. The word comes from the same root as *vital*, but it moves in the opposite direction, away from what God has created and called good and blessed. Violence misuses the gift of life, trading it for some dull or brassy idol that promises control, predictability, or certainty. That brassy idol is simply a dressed up and tricked out phantasm of death. The life God has created is free to choose—and it can choose life or death. Violence seeks to steal that freedom or end it. Violence can be an instinctive reaction to preserve life when other violence threatens—like attacking a charging animal likely to maim vulnerable children. Violence can also be a more or less conscious choice that seeks to augment life at the cost of others—the assassination of a political opponent, or the crazed mayhem of an unstable shooter.

We often try to counter violence by superior violence or by fencing it in. Jesus teaches another way.

The nuns in the convent school I attended as a child taught us custody of the eyes—being conscious about what we see, and turning away from distractions that prevent us from seeing the presence of the holy. Sometimes we need to avoid seeing what is unhelpful or unedifying or because it may harm another. But it's also about seeing what needs to be noticed, either for praise or correction. Do you remember Shug telling Celie, "I think it [ticks] God off when you walk by the color purple in a field and don't notice."[9] Custody of the eyes is about cultivating a kind of purity of seeing, a perfection that avoids aggressive possession as well as defensiveness. It can be misused—in the overly guarded vision that refuses to see a neighbor in need, or as we were also taught by those nuns to avoid playing with Protestant children lest we be tainted or misled.

Countering violence requires custody of the heart. Violence begins in the heart, especially in hearts that have been wounded and scarred by the violence of others, and then react and respond aggressively, in overly defended ways. Violence begins in the heart that cannot countenance vulnerability—rooted in fear that its own vitality will be extinguished. As the counterforce to abundant life, violence is intrinsically kin to evil.

The ultimate counterforce to fear is perfect love, the ability to share life to the full, with radical vulnerability, in the face of those who would destroy it. The undefended Jesus shows us the way. He does not go about with armies or weapons, he does not protest the words of his captors, he does not defend himself or attack others with violent words or actions, and it is ultimately his ability to set his life force and spirit free, fully free, that deprives the evil around him of any ultimate power.

Vulnerability is finally galvanizing those of us who are less than perfect into action—through the slaughter of innocents in our schools and on our streets, and the willingness to let our hearts bear some of that pain. The civil rights struggles of this nation,

---

9   Alice Walker, *The Color Purple* (New York: Hartcourt Brace Jovanovich, 1982).

and the wanton violence of others, even those charged to uphold the law, finally galvanized the passive people of this nation into active response. Response in the face of lynchings, cross burnings, fire hoses, and attack dogs. That active response is most effective when it is nonviolent and openly vulnerable.

It looks like the widow, showing up day after day to ask for justice. It is Paul urging, "Do not repay anyone evil for evil. . . . Never avenge yourselves. . . . No, 'if your enemies are hungry, feed them; if they are thirsty, give them something to drink; for by doing this you heap burning coals on their heads.' Do not be overcome by evil, but overcome evil with good."[10] I believe Paul means burning coals not as vengeance, but the coal the angels use to touch Isaiah's lips, and remove his guilt and sin.[11]

Nonviolence is ultimately the only creative response, for an absence of life cannot bring about greater life. Feeding the rage of violence may briefly burn out the heart of aggression, but it only increases the carnage. It does not increase love.

Custody of the heart is what Jimmy Carter was talking about when he said that he'd committed adultery many times in his heart. We commit violence when we judge others less than ourselves, when we wish them ill, when we give them labels that serve to prejudge or dismiss them. Peacemaking begins in the depths of our hearts, by loving those we first address as enemies.

Enemy literally means "not a friend." Acting out of love begins to change that. It begins in our hearts, in response to threat and stranger, and it moves out across families, communities, and nations. If the immediate response to perceived threat is an attempt to destroy, we are no better than the beasts. When we can "be not anxious," we just might meet Jesus in this one who is not yet known as friend.

Custody does not mean closing up your heart—it means setting boundaries on how the heart responds. It's more like stewardship, guarding and keeping watch. It is aided by remembering—even by rehearsing—that we are God's beloved and God is well pleased with us, and with every other human creature on this earth, and that God has given abundance for the good of all creation.

Custody of the heart is a spiritual discipline that unleashes the power of love and abundant life. In the midst of the Irish troubles forty years ago, instead of praying that God turn an enemy's ankle, I discovered that I was being led to pray for Ian Paisley. At the

---

10   Romans 12:17, 19, 20–21.
11   Isaiah 6:6–7.

time he seemed to me an image of evil incarnate. But that discipline changed my heart. When a stranger grabbed me when I was out running a couple of years ago, I yelled and wrestled with him until we reached a stalemate. It finally dawned on me that putting my foot in a sensitive place might induce him to let go—and it did, without damage to either of us. At another time in my life I think I might have tried to hurt him before I realized that he was mentally ill, that I had somehow entered his zone of safety and threatened him. I still wish that I had been present enough to hug him rather than running away.

Consider how violence was transfigured in the shooting in Nickel Mines, Pennsylvania—the story known to many of us through *Amish Grace*.[12] The community forgave, reconciled, and rebuilt their schoolhouse, naming it New Hope. The memorial site in this city [Oklahoma City] has begun to turn swords into plowshares by planting a garden, letting water flow in the desert, and remembering and celebrating the unique gifts of each vulnerable and beloved child of God who died in that place.

Countering violence begins in our hearts—with the words we choose, the judgments we make, and the vulnerability we're willing to assume. We stand at the gate of Holy Week. Before us is the cosmic example of the prince of peace, who befriends the world, and meets the world's violence with love.

> Deep peace of the running wave to you.
> Deep peace of the flowing air to you.
> Deep peace of the quiet earth to you.
> Deep peace of the shining stars to you.
> Deep peace of the infinite peace to you.
> Deep peace of Christ to you.
> Deep peace of the prince of peace to you—and through you, to the world.[13]

The Most Reverend Katharine Jefferts Schori is the twenty-sixth presiding bishop of the Episcopal Church. She has been vocal about the Episcopal Church's mission priorities, including the United

---

12   Donald B. Kraybill, *Amish Grace: How Forgiveness Transcended Tragedy* (San Francisco: Jossey-Bass, 2010).

13   Traditional Celtic blessing.

Nations Millennium Development Goals, issues of domestic poverty, climate change and care for the earth, as well as the ongoing need to contextualize the gospel. She preached this sermon at St. Paul's Cathedral in Oklahoma City on Friday, April 11, 2014, at the closing Eucharist of "Reclaiming the Gospel of Peace."

For Reflection

1. Where is your story in this story?
2. Where do you see God?
3. What causes you to pause and rethink your previous assumptions?
4. What cries out to you?
5. What calls to you?

Go Deeper

1. How could you cultivate and practice "custody of the eyes"?
2. How could you cultivate and practice "custody of the heart"?

6

The Binding of Isaac

Allison S. Liles

The binding of Isaac or the *akedah* is one of those biblical stories that some of us wish would just disappear. There are several upsetting stories like this in Hebrew Scripture—stories of betrayal and infidelity, of racism and murder, of rape and genocide. They are not the warm, fuzzy stories of the Gospels. These stories make us uncomfortable. They make us question the nature of our loving God. However, most of these stories touch on realities about ourselves and our common humanity that both confuse and terrify us . . . which is why we keep coming back to them.

Our story today from Genesis 22:1–14 is certainly among these shocking and horrifying texts. When we hear it we instinctively ask ourselves how anyone could seriously consider killing his or her own child to please God. We wonder how anyone could believe that God would ask a person to kill a child. And if we are brave enough, we may begin asking ourselves what kind of god would test someone by asking them to kill a child, and whether this could really be the God that we worship.

These questions are important, but before I try answering them, there are a couple other items that need addressing. The first is that these questions arise from our personal horror over the idea of sacrificing children, but such questions would not have arisen when this story was first told. In Abraham's day and in

34

the generations following when this story was retold, the religious sacrifice of children was not much of a shock. The fact that later laws found in Leviticus[14] explicitly prohibiting the offering of children as religious sacrifices shows that the practice was common enough to need addressing. So rather than provoke shock, this story originally served as part of the explanation for why the Israelites, unlike worshipers of other gods, did not sacrifice children.

The other thing to note is that a major reason we have trouble with this story is that so many of us approach it first with the assumption that these stories actually happened. When we read it literally, guilt paralyzes us, as we know we could never pass such a test of faith. When we read it literally we are overwhelmed with horror over a God that nearly lets a father take a knife to his beloved son. We instead should approach this story first with the assumption that it has something to teach us about ourselves and about God. And only then should we question whether or not it actually took place.

So what does it have to teach us? The narrative states that, "God tested Abraham." It doesn't state what the test sought to discover, but I think God was seeking to find out for what Abraham would sacrifice his child. You see, as much as we are disturbed by the idea of child sacrifices, the truth is that today in modern-day America people sacrifice their children all the time. Our country routinely decides that there are causes worth sacrificing our children. We are on the brink of yet another war in which our government will have to decide if the ultimate goal of peace in Iraq is worth sacrificing young men and women. We're on the brink of another war in which children will be lumped into the "collateral damage" category of drone warfare. An estimated three hundred thousand American children have been sacrificed to sexual human trafficking. And then there are the staggering numbers of children sacrificed so that adults can continue embracing their constitutional right to bear arms. The Brady Campaign to Prevent Gun Violence[15] reports that eight children are sacrificed on the altar of the gun every single day in our country. From accidental shootings by adults to children who gain access to unsecured guns to gang violence, suicide, and the all-too-common school shootings—an estimated ten thousand children are shot each year. And for what? So we the people of the United States can stock up on military-style

---

14   Leviticus 18:21 and 20:1–2.

15   www.bradycampaign.org.

weapons? So we can have a personal arsenal of semiautomatic guns in our homes? So we can overthrow the government?

Like Abraham trudging up the hill to Mt. Moriah, we have been fooled into believing that the only way to appease the angry and demanding gun-god is by accepting that our children must be sacrificed. We unquestioningly believe in the ritual practice of manufacturing more and more guns. We continue to give unfettered access to these weapons so they can be used as "protection." But, in fact, the opposite is true. The more guns we produce and sell, the more people who have them, the more children who are sacrificed.

In the Genesis story, Abraham and Isaac begin their final walk to the site of sacrifice. Isaac's mind must have been racing, the weight of the wood on his shoulders, the weight of the pit of his stomach as he looks around for the sheep. If Isaac is old enough to carry the wood, he is old enough to understand what is happening. Finally he asks, "Father, the fire and the wood are here, but where is the lamb?" His question must have brought Abraham to tears; Abraham can barely answer the boy. He simply says, "The Lord will provide the lamb."

When I talk to my five-year-old son Hill about the school shootings that happen nearly every single week of the academic year, I am reminded of Isaac's words. Hill nearly always asks me, "Mommy, will bad guys come to my school?" And each time he says this I hear him asking, "Mommy, am I the lamb to be sacrificed?" It always brings me to tears and like Abraham I can barely choke out my answer, "I pray that it won't. I pray that God will provide, but I just don't know." I should not be scared to send my child to elementary school in August and yet I am because children have become something worth sacrificing so that our country can continue bearing arms.

God's question was not "would Abraham be prepared to sacrifice his child," but "for what would Abraham be prepared to sacrifice his child?" And surely that is the question of us, too. What are we willing to sacrifice to continue in this relationship with God? What are we willing to sacrifice to continue in relationship with all the other gods in our life?

The story of the binding of Isaac teaches us that God does not demand the blood of children. God tell us not to sacrifice our children. Not now, not ever. When the voice of the Lord, the God of justice and compassion, cries out, "Do not lay your hand on the boy or do anything to him" Abraham responds in obedience and faithfulness. And that is where this story is calling us today: to be faithful to God and to our children by refusing to sacrifice them to the gods to whom everyone else is sacrificing their children. When the gods of guns, war, greed, and selfish ambition demand that we sacrifice our children, we must have the courage and integrity to resist them. We must instead obey the voice crying out "Stop! Do not lay a hand on the child." We are called to choose—to choose between a God of violence and a God who comes to us embodied in a child.

The Reverend Allison S. Liles is the executive director of the Episcopal Peace Fellowship. A graduate of Virginia Theological Seminary in 2006, she preached this sermon based on Genesis 22:1–14 (Proper 8A) at St. Paul's Memorial Church in Charlottesville, Virginia, on June 29, 2014.

For Reflection

1. Where is your story in this story?
2. Where do you see God?
3. What causes you to pause and rethink your previous assumptions?
4. What cries out to you?
5. What calls to you?

Go Deeper

1. How do you "sacrifice" your children, friends, or family?
2. What are the "gods" in your life?
3. What are you willing to sacrifice to continue your relationship with these "other gods" in your life?
4. What are you willing to sacrifice to continue your relationship with God?

SUSTAIN:
THE WITNESS

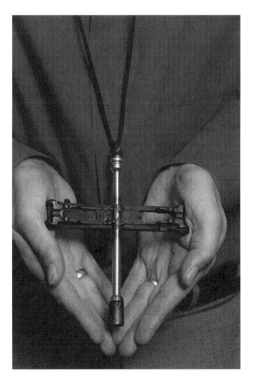

The pectoral cross of the Right Reverend James E. Curry given to him by the Anglican Diocese of Lebombo in Mozambique. The upright of the cross is the piston of the automatic action of an AK-47 and the arms of the cross are made from the sight mounts of the AK-47. Photo ©2014 Marc Yves Regis. Used with permission.

7

What Shall We Do?

Mariann Edgar Budde

And the crowd asked [John the Baptist], "What then should we do?" (Luke 3:10)

I spoke with the Episcopal bishop of Connecticut on Friday morning. He had called to ask me a routine question, and we chatted amicably for about twenty minutes. He mentioned news of a school shooting, but he didn't have specific information yet. "It's a harsh world, Mariann," he said, and I agreed. We hung up, after which he surely received the wrenching particulars of the events in Newtown that sent him and his colleagues to offer whatever help they could.

Rabbi Shaul Praver of Temple Adath Israel of Newtown was interviewed on Public Radio yesterday. He was among the religious leaders who sat in a nearby firehouse with families waiting to be reunited with their children. As the numbers of waiting families diminished in number, their panic increased, and each religious leader was assigned to a family. We can only imagine the collective anguish when officials announced that all the as yet unaccounted for children didn't make it. The rabbi's task was to console a mother who lost her first-grade son.

"What did you say?" the interviewer asked, "I told her," the rabbi responded, "that I believe in the eternity of the soul and that I believed that she would see her son again someday. But that was my only theological statement; mainly I was there to help her simply to survive each wrenching moment of that horrible day."

"I don't have the answer to why these things happen," he said. "I've never liked theological answers in the face of suffering. As religious people we can't solve these things like a math equation. We can only share the suffering of our fellow human beings and offer whatever compassion we can."

The interview ended with Rabbi Praver asking us all to pray. "The silent prayers of your listeners," he said, "will help these families in this horrible time."

And so we pray, not at all certain that our prayers help. Prayer is an instinctual response in times such as these, whether we call that response prayer or not. We pray in anguish, or anger, or more often than not, in numb incomprehension. In the words of a friend and father of two young sons, "It's hard to find the right words. Or think the right thoughts. Or feel the right pain. Everything is so wrong."

Invariably, a question arises from our prayer, one that echoes across time and space, the question human beings always ask in the face of suffering or injustice or collective sin. It's the same question that those who flocked to John the Baptizer asked so many years ago: *What shall we do?*

John's answer is noteworthy for its simplicity. First he said, "Bear fruits worthy of repentance." In other words, regret alone isn't enough. He called on people to change their lives in meaningful, measurable ways. "Bear *fruits*." When people wanted to know specifically what they should do, he said, in essence, *do what you already know is right*. If you have more than you need, share with those who don't have enough. If you hold power over another, do not abuse that power. If you are a soldier, do not use your weapons for personal gain. Be honest and decent and at peace with what you have.

What do you suppose John would say were we to ask him, "In light of the darkest Friday we can imagine, what shall *we* do?" Surely he would he look us in the eye and say, "Bear fruits worthy of repentance, worthy of your sorrow, worthy of those who lost their lives and their precious ones. And do what you already know is right."

On September 18, 1963, just one month after his triumphant "I Have a Dream" speech on the steps of the Lincoln Memorial, the Reverend Dr. Martin Luther King Jr. preached at the funeral of three young girls—Addie Mae Collins, Carol Denise McNair, and Cynthia Diane Wesley—who were killed by a bomb as they attended Sunday school of the 16th Street Baptist Church in Birmingham, Alabama. He said:

> This afternoon we gather in the quiet of this sanctuary to pay our last tribute of respect to these beautiful children of God. They entered the stage of history just a few years ago, and in the brief years that they were privileged to act on this mortal stage, they played their parts exceedingly well. Now the curtain falls; they move through the exit; the drama of their earthly life comes to a close. They are now committed back to that eternity from which they came.
>
> These children—unoffending, innocent, and beautiful—were the victims of one of the most vicious and tragic crimes ever perpetrated against humanity. And yet they died nobly. They are the martyred heroines of a holy crusade for freedom and human dignity. And so they have something to say to each of us in their death. They have something to say to every minister of the gospel who has remained silent behind the safe security of stained-glass windows. They have something to say to every politician who has fed his constituents with the stale bread of hatred and the spoiled meat of racism. They have something to say to every Negro who has passively accepted the evil system of segregation and who has stood on the sidelines in a mighty struggle for justice.
>
> They say to each of us, black and white alike, that we must substitute courage for caution. They say to us that we must be concerned not merely about who murdered them, but about the system, the way of life, the philosophy which produced the murderers. Their death says to us that we must work passionately and unrelentingly for the realization of the American dream. And so my friends, they did not die in vain. God still has a way of wringing good out of evil. And history has proven over and over again that unmerited suffering is redemptive. The innocent blood of these little girls may well serve as a redemptive force that will bring new light to this dark city.[16]

---

16 Martin Luther King Jr., "Eulogy for the Martyred Children" delivered September 18, 1963.

I suggest to you that we must resolve, as a nation, not to allow the Newtown children and their teachers to die in vain. If we only pray and do not bear fruits worthy of repentance and do what we know to be right, we dishonor them. If we only pray and do not act, we are complicit in perpetuating the conditions that allow such crimes to occur. It is time, once again, to substitute courage for caution.

I, for one, have decided to join forces with Dean Hall at the National Cathedral and all people of faith and good will who are saying now, in response to Friday's tragedy, that enough is enough. We have been fed enough the stale bread of violence. We have been complicit too long in a system that allows such crimes to continue. Since 1979, 119,079 children and teens have been killed by gun violence, according to Marian Wright Edelman of the Children's Defense Fund, more than the number of Americans killed in any of the twentieth century's largest wars. More than ten thousand Americans were killed by gun violence last year alone.

Dean Hall and I have decided to dedicate ourselves to the work of passing national legislation to ban the sale of assault weapons and ammunition in this country and I invite you, as a congregation, to join us and others for whom something snapped inside on Friday, as if we collectively all awoke from a very bad dream. While there are legitimate reasons to own a gun for sport and self-defense, there is no reason for civilians to own weapons whose only purpose is to kill large numbers of people. And while there is far more to be done to reduce violence in our nation and to care for the mentally ill, if we don't begin with the most obvious first steps, how will we ever progress to more difficult challenges?

A television reporter asked me yesterday if I thought, as he did, that this shooting might be the one to strengthen national resolve to address gun violence, given the slaughter of innocents in the midst of a holy season, I said yes, surely, for those reasons. And there is also this political reality: we occupy the briefest of moments now, when our political leaders are not under the immediate pressure of an election. Now the powerful influence of the gun lobby could be met and matched, in the words of Dean Hall, by the power of the cross lobby. "Our political leaders need to know," he is saying in his sermon this morning, "that there is a group of people in America who will serve as a counterweight to the gun lobby, who will stand together and support them as they act to take assault weapons off the streets. As followers of Jesus, we are led by one who died at the hand of human violence. We know something about innocent suffering. And we know our job is to heal it and stop it wherever we can." It is time—past time—to take the first meaningful step in ending the epidemic of gun violence in this country.

I'd like to say a personal word to those being confirmed this morning and who are being received into the Episcopal Church. First, I want to thank you for taking this important spiritual step, saying to God, yourselves, and this community that you want to stand and be counted, that you choose to be part of a spiritual tradition inspired by the living spirit of Jesus, and that you promise to live your lives in a manner worthy of him. You are about to make promises of great significance, and to receive a blessing that will remain with you for the rest of your lives. It is the blessing of the Holy Spirit that already resides within you, joining with your spirit, enabling you to live fully into your God-given gifts and to extraordinary things for the sake of love. And your decision to stand tall gives us all the opportunity to renew our baptismal promises alongside you.

Among the promises we renew together are these: "Will we persevere in resisting evil? Will we proclaim by word and example the Good News of God in Christ? Will we seek and serve Christ in all persons? Will we strive for justice and peace among all people?" And we respond, "We will, with God's help."

Like the good rabbi of Newtown I do believe in the eternity of souls, but as a mother I know that would be no consolation today. I believe that our silent prayers are of help to those who mourn, but like Martin Luther King Jr., I also believe that the time has come to substitute courage for caution, bear fruits worthy of deep sorrow, and act so that those precious ones lost on Friday will not have died in vain.

The Right Reverend Mariann Edgar Budde was consecrated the ninth bishop of the Diocese of Washington in November 2011. This sermon was preached at St. Alban's Episcopal Church in Washington, DC, on the Third Sunday of Advent, December 16, 2012, in which the rite of Confirmation was celebrated.

For Reflection

1. Where is your story in this story?
2. Where do you see God?

3. What causes you to pause and rethink your previous assumptions?
4. What cries out to you?
5. What calls to you?

Go Deeper

1. In times of anguish, how do you "bear fruits worthy of repentance, worthy of sorrow" and "do what you already know is right"?
2. How is prayer and action connected? Can you have one without the other?
3. How do you live into the baptismal promise of resisting evil?
4. How do you live into the baptismal promise of proclaiming by word and example the Good News of God in Christ?
5. How do you live into the baptismal promise of seeking and serving Christ in all persons?
6. How do you live into the baptismal promise of striving for justice and peace among all people?

Render Our Hearts Open

Kathleen Adams-Shepherd

Thank you for the invitation to share a few reflections with you this morning and far more importantly I thank those who planned the time and space for this critical discussion together, those who have shared and implemented, all of you who have given time over to this work with Holy Week immediately before us, the good people who work here who have tended to us and cleaned up after us, the archbishop and presiding bishop, the bishop and people of the Diocese of Oklahoma, and the bishop of Maryland. It is a very important part of the healing process for every person touched by violence and by violent death that we come together from all corners of life and faith and belief and perspective seeking a way—seeking multiple ways—to live as co-missioners with God to reclaim the Gospel of Peace.

I am standing here this morning because the violence that takes the lives of God's beloved children every day all over our country and world visited us in all of its horrific and tragic loss in the quiet suburb of Newtown, Connecticut, on December 14, 2012. Twenty-eight lives were violently and tragically cut short by a mentally ill young man who had access to the kinds of weapons and high capacity magazines that he simply should never have had at his disposal, but rather should have had access to affirming mental health support. And even though the tragedy in

Sandy Hook shook the world as Archbishop Welby has said—and many have said was a tipping point for people of faith at least—we in Newtown are quite aware that we joined a large part of the world who suffer with merciless frequency from violence and terrorism that take loved ones every day. We have been visited *by* and we have visited *with* many people who have lost loved ones violently at the hand of another in this country and around the world. The utter loss, pain, and grief have brought us together. I am sorry that it took such a tragedy in an affluent community in one of the wealthiest counties in this first-world country to wake us up even just enough to have conversations like this one. The horrific and violent deaths of our brothers and sisters and all our children all over the world for all these years should have been equally compelling, and perhaps now they are.

I admit to you that before December 14, 2012, I grieved and prayed over so many deaths by violence. But it was not until I saw and felt firsthand its devastation that I began to commit myself to advocacy and partnership with those who witness daily to that proclamation of peace that is at the heart of our gathering here.

The witnesses preceding me in this time together have given us much to consider as we ponder the causes of this epidemic of violence—as our confession so clearly says, "We repent of the evil that enslaves us, the evil we have done, and the evil done on our behalf. . . ." I shudder there—so much evil done that I have still to confront—to lend my convictions, faith, and vows to—no life lost is more important than another.

Much has already been so well said about our violent tendencies and propensities, and the theology of vows (if kept) that would certainly change our epidemic culture of violence into one of dignity and respect for the incarnate God who dwells in each and every human being—friend, enemy, or somewhere in-between. Every human life.

What I want to say in the midst of this urgent work of reclaiming the Gospel of Peace is a word of hope. In one commentary it is written:

> In Joel, the Judeans are threatened with death by their present catastrophe and by the day of the Lord's coming, but God nevertheless offers them the opportunity to repent and to return to communion with God. As a sign of their sincere willingness to return, Joel instructs the people to hold a fast of lamentation, in which the priests, praying on behalf of the people and themselves, plead for

God's mercy. In the midst of Judah's desperate situation, occasioned by locust plague and drought, and with a final, awful judgment hanging over it, God utters a "but." God calls the Judeans to return to worship with all their hearts and to rend their hearts and not their garments. As we know, the tearing of garments in lamentation was an expression of deep emotion in times of grief, terror, or horror at some misfortune, but the expression of repentance in Judah's heart is to be even more emphatic. The heart in Hebrew idiom symbolizes what the brain symbolizes in our language today. The heart was understood as the seat of the will and intellect, so that Judah is being asked to turn away from apostasy and return to God in a deliberate act of will. To repent or turn to God has the meaning of "turning around" of willing ourselves to go in the opposite direction, so that we are leading a life far different from what went before.[17]

The verse we shared this morning from Joel [2:13] and the verses on either side of it reveals how long suffering and patient our God is with those in covenant with God. But even now, in this untenable situation we find ourselves standing in—this culture of violence, even now the offer to turn around, to repent, to rend our hearts open, to receive and offer God's love to all humanity—the offer to return to fellowship with our God is held out to *us.*

It is that little "but" that makes all the difference. That God refuses to be done with us is utterly amazing to me. God's unwavering yearning to bring us into life, not death, is our hope. God's love for us runs so deep that God refuses to accept our evil ways as the end of us and is determined to forgive us and welcome us back every time we turn around—rending our hearts, tearing them open, and letting God enter anew with the strength needed to will ourselves to love as God loves us. Right in the very midst of doom, there is hope. And for Joel, repentance is not just an *individual* act of piety, it is the role and calling of the entire community of faith.

The conversations of these few days, the conversations I have been invited into time and time again since December 2012,

---

17   Elizabeth Achtemeier, Robert A. Bennett, Francisco O. García-Treto, Donald E. Gowan, Theodore Hiebert, W. Eugene March, Frederick J. Murphy, Ben C. Ollenburger, Samuel Pagán, Eileen M. Schuller, Daniel J. Simundson, Daniel L. Smith-Christopher, Phyllis Trible, and Gale A. Yee, contributors, *The New Interpreter's Bible Commentary* (Nashville: Abingdon Press, 1996), 7:318-19.

the outcry near and far is getting louder. It certainly may take some patience, steady commitment, and true agape for all God's people from each of us, but it does feel that we are in the midst of the rending of our hearts and God is in us determined that we should succeed.

I repent that it took such horrific loss in my own life, ministry, and community to help me understand more fully my own complicity and my call. I am exhausted from shared grief but energized by the shared rending of our hearts.

In the nearly sixteen months since the tragedy in Sandy Hook there have been clear signs of God's determination to wrestle light from utter darkness. God is planting in our hearts a deep desire to connect with others who suffer tragedy, natural or human made. We brought a group of teenagers right here to Oklahoma last summer; teens from various faith backgrounds and no faith backgrounds, who came to help with the cleanup in Moore and the reconstruction work in Norman. We met with several of the families who lost children in the tornado that leveled the Plaza Hill Elementary School and our common grief connected us in love. We are taking another group of teens to Colorado this summer to help with the flood cleanup. We have a new companion relationship with San Jose La Montana in El Salvador, which is connecting us to a people who have long suffered much agony and loss and are rebuilding home, life, and community with an unwavering faith. We are working closely with Lumiere La DeMain in Haiti to support the education of all Haiti's children; our youth continue to work with John Dau, a leader of the Lost Boys of the Sudan, now a grown man living in the United States who has built a hospital in the Sudan, helping fund a midwife and the digging of two wells in his homeland at his request through the Hope of Sudan.

The tragedy has drawn us together with the people of the world as we live into the call to seek and serve Christ in all persons and respect the dignity of every human being and their right to live and prosper free of oppression with access to all the things we often take for granted. This horrible tragedy has called us to work for sensible gun laws, affirming mental health support for all who need it, the safety of all God's children, and the welfare of all God's people. God is working in us not only that we might find healing for ourselves, but that we might grow in faith as we are connected to people in the midst of healing all over the world. Indeed the world has gotten smaller for us, and our hearts so much larger.

After the tragedy in Sandy Hook a colleague sent me a piece written by Thomas Long in *The Christian Century* and it has spoken to me so poignantly in these months. He wrote:

> Beyond this, the larger notion that grief moves through some kind of process toward resolution probably owes more of a debt to American optimism than to the hope of faith. Grief is not mainly a psychotherapeutic unfolding; it is a perilous, unruly, and emotionally fraught narrative task. We are all players in a human drama, mundane mostly but also filled with grandeur and deep pathos. When someone dies, the plot threads unravel, the narrative shatters, and those of us who are part of the story "go to pieces." The work of grief is to gather the fragments and to rewrite the narrative, this time minus a treasured presence.
>
> But we do not do this alone. In the wilderness of grief, God provides narrative manna, just enough shape and meaning to keep us walking, and sends the Comforter, who knits together the raveled soul and refuses to leave us orphaned. Sometimes the bereaved say they are looking for closure, but we people of faith do not seek closure so much, as we pray that all our lost loves will be gathered into the great unending story fashioned by God's grace.[18]

Let us pray: We thank you gracious and loving God, for those who have gone before us and now live in that place of eternal life. You help us learn as you work mightily to transform such loss that in every season of life and death you are near us, standing firm in love when we falter and offering that holy "but" that calls us to rend our hearts and return to you. We long for the time when your own hand will dry all our tears and your own love will reknit our story into your story of peace with one another. Be our companion in these days, our path on the way, and our hope for a new fabric of life, a new narrative that will be one of courage and conviction to work to make this new story one of love for all humanity—a place within our mending hearts and aching lives where the veil

---

18   Thomas Long, "Grief Without Stages," *The Christian Century* 128, no. 3 (June 28, 2011): 20–21.

between this world and the next will tear and your love which dwells within us will bring us all together in your great goodness. "Pour upon us wisdom, courage and compassionate energy to witness to your love. Open our mouths to speak and our lives to act in ways that affirm, build up, and rejoice in every one of your children. Give us a voice to call for just laws, for an end to hatred and violence, for ready access to mental health services, and for dialogue filled with respect and careful listening. Let us never ignore any life lost and never cease to witness to your love until all are safe and living in peace."[19] Be our constant companion, our path on the way, and our hope for tomorrow. And let us ever be reminded that, in the words of Henri-Frederic Amiel, "Life is short, and we do not have much time to gladden the hearts of those who travel with us. So let us be quick to love and make haste to be kind." In the name of our God who welcomes us home and calls us to the work of peace. Amen.

The Reverend Kathleen "Kathie" Adams-Shepherd has served as the rector of Trinity Episcopal Church in Newtown, Connecticut, since 1996, having previously ministered at churches in Oswego, Clayton, and Cape Vincent in New York State. She is a graduate of Union Theological Seminary in New York City. This reflection was given during Morning Prayer on April 9, 2014, at "Reclaiming the Gospel of Peace" in Oklahoma City.

For Reflection

1. Where is your story in this story?
2. Where do you see God?
3. What causes you to pause and rethink your previous assumptions?
4. What cries out to you?
5. What calls to you?

---

19   The Episcopal Church in Connecticut, *The Way of the Cross: Challenging a Culture of Violence* (Hartford, CT: Episcopal Church in Connecticut, 2013), 5. https://www. episcopalct.org/Beliefs-and-Practices/Challenging-Violence/

Go Deeper

1. How do you respond to the call to rend your heart, instead of tearing your garments?
2. How are you (or your community) called to repent in the wake of violence in our society?
3. What are you called to work for?
4. How have you experienced the narrative manna of God?

9

The Unruly Wills and Affections of Sinners[20]

Gary R. Hall

Our Gospel for today [John 12:1–8] tells the story of a party where things went horribly wrong. In this account, Jesus goes to the house of Mary and Martha of Bethany, the sisters of Lazarus. Lazarus is the man Jesus raised from the dead. His sisters have personalities remarkably different from each other. In the most well-known story (Luke 10:38–42), Martha works slavishly in the kitchen while Mary sits at Jesus's feet and listens to his teaching. Surprisingly to many of us, that encounter ends better for Mary than it does for Martha. Jesus says, "Martha, Martha, you are worried and distracted by many things; there is need of only one thing. Mary has chosen the better part, which will not be taken away from her" (Luke 10:41–42). But that's another sermon.

In today's passage, Jesus is attending a dinner at the Bethany house when Mary, seemingly for no reason at all, takes a jar of expensive ointment and uses it to anoint his feet. The fragrance

---

20 "Almighty God, you alone can bring into order the unruly wills and affections of sinners: Grant your people grace to love what you command and desire what you promise; that, among the swift and varied changes of the world, our hearts may surely there be fixed where true joys are to be found; through Jesus Christ our Lord, who lives and reigns with you and the Holy Spirit, one God, now and for ever. Amen." (Collect for the Fifth Sunday of Lent, Book of Common Prayer, 219).

of the perfume fills the room, but the smell does not quiet the attendant passions. Judas—the Zealot who will ultimately betray Jesus—loses his temper. "Why was this perfume not sold for three hundred denarii and the money given to the poor?" Just as Jesus had admonished Martha in the earlier story when she complained that Mary was not helping her serve the meal, so in this moment Jesus steps in and chastises Judas, "Leave her alone. She bought it so that she might keep it for the day of my burial. You always have the poor with you, but you do not always have me." Like the Smothers Brothers' mom, Jesus always seems to like Mary best.

Let's try to imagine the dysfunction of this dinner party. Martha is slaving away in the kitchen, her sister Mary is anointing Jesus's feet, and Judas is pitching a fit because he disagrees with Mary's fiscal priorities. Then the authority figure steps in and sides with one of them against the other. This is like the worst Thanksgiving dinner you can imagine. I get a stomachache every time I read this story. Before you know it, the perfect evening has gone all to hell.

So that's one bad party. I want to talk now about another one where things went even worse. It happened not in Bible times but in 1993 in the Park La Brea section of Los Angeles. Adam Scott, a twenty-seven-year old man, had recently graduated from USC Law School and had just begun work at a downtown law firm. He was at a party at a friend's house when the host invited a group of guests into his bedroom to see his gun collection. The host wanted to show off his new 12-gauge semiautomatic shotgun, and he first pointed it at another guest, saying it wasn't loaded. Then he pointed the shotgun at Adam Scott. The gun went off. The young lawyer, hit once in the head, died within minutes.

According to witnesses, immediately before his shooting, Adam Scott had said, "I don't even think I could fire a gun in self-defense."[21]

I didn't know Adam Scott, but I did and still do know his parents, Jack and Lacreta, quite well. At the time of his son's death, Jack was president of Pasadena City College, and the Scotts were active, faithful members of All Saints Church in Pasadena, where I served at the time of Adam's death. Not long after the shooting, Jack resigned his college job and committed the rest of his working life to curbing gun violence. He spent the next sixteen years in the California State Assembly and State Senate working tirelessly in that effort.

---

21   Renee Tawa. "Slayings Put Educator on Crusade for Gun Control," *Los Angeles Times,* November 21, 1993.

The events of the past year—the mass shootings in Newtown, Connecticut, and Aurora, Colorado, the avalanche of daily killings in Chicago and elsewhere—have rightly galvanized the faith community to speak and act in pastoral response to these tragedies. People die daily in America as a result of human malevolence. But today's Gospel and the story of Adam Scott point us toward another reality: people die not only because of evil intentions. People die because we are not always in control of our own behavior. Despite our best efforts, we are always in danger of finding ourselves at an event where things suddenly and tragically go wrong.

None of us is in control of the actions of others. None of us is entirely in control of our own actions. The problem is what our prayer book calls "the unruly wills and affections of sinners," and our prayer for today asks that God not only bring order to that seemingly uncontrollable part of us, it also pleads that God grant us grace to love what God commands and desire what God promises.

I don't know about you, but I recognize myself in that prayer. My wills and affections are unruly. And though I may strive to obey God's commands, I don't always love them. And if that's true for me, it's probably true for all of us. We're like the guests at the Bethany dinner with Jesus: we're out of control, selfish, and prone to make mistakes. In the words of the late Rodney King, "Can we all just get along?"

Here at Washington National Cathedral we have spent the last several days observing a Gun Violence Prevention Sabbath Weekend. We are doing this in collaboration with our partner organization, Faiths United to Prevent Gun Violence and with more than two hundred faith communities across America. Since Thursday night, we have gathered to pray, reflect, listen, learn, and commit ourselves to action that will help bring this epidemic to an end.

Taken together, today's Gospel and the story of Adam Scott sketch the outlines of gun violence as a religious problem. Like all violence, gun violence will plague us as long as the wills and affections of sinners continue to be unruly. Mary and Martha and Judas turn a dinner with Jesus into a family argument. A young man goes to a party and ends up dead. These things don't happen only because of human ill will. They happen because none of us is, finally, in control of ourselves. Our wills and affections are unruly. We neither love what God commands nor desire what God promises. That is the human condition: we may think we're in charge, but when we're honest with ourselves we know that much of the time we're out of control both personally and socially. In the Christian tradition, we call that condition "sin," and we give over the season of Lent to lamenting it, examining it, and working together to find new ways to live with it even as we move, with Jesus, into God's future.

Gun violence will continue to be a religious problem as long as people like you and me are sinners. When we say that we're sinners, we do not say that in a negative or judgmental way. We say it in recognition of the way things are. I don't always know what's best for myself. I want what I want, often regardless of the consequences. My judgment is limited and finite and partial. Real spiritual and psychological health begins with an acknowledgement of my situation. "All we like sheep have gone astray" (Isaiah 53:6). That's what the Bible means when it calls us sinners: not that we're bad, merely that we're cosmically accident-prone. God doesn't love us in spite of our sinfulness. God loves us in full knowledge of who we are and of what we are capable.

When Martha and Judas complain about Mary's contemplative attention to Jesus, they are not being evil, merely mistaken. We need to work together to lessen the occurrence of gun deaths not because people are evil but because we're neither as smart nor invulnerable as we like to think ourselves. We need each other to make our way through life. That's what society, that's what the church, is all about. And that's why we at Washington National Cathedral are in this gun violence work for the long haul. We won't give up until our streets and our schools and our children are safe. We owe at least that much to our children, our neighbors, ourselves.

As perfect as we try to make them, our dinners, our parties, all our efforts will always contain within them the possibility of going horribly wrong. At first, that may sound like bad news. But there is good news, too. As dysfunctional as our gatherings may be, Jesus will still always manage to come to them. We may go astray, but we are not abandoned in our confusion, our sinfulness, our vulnerability. Jesus is here among us now as we gather at his table. He calls us not only to love and forgive and accept ourselves and each other. He calls us also to help him make a world where all God's precious children will be safe from violence in all its forms. All we like sheep have gone astray, are going astray, will continue to go astray. But we do have a shepherd in Jesus, and for that one's loving gracious care for each and all of us we gather at his table to give thanks. Amen.

The Very Reverend Gary R. Hall has been the tenth dean of Washington National Cathedral since 2012. He was dean and president of Seabury-Western Theological Seminary in Evanston, Illinois, from 2005 to 2010 and has served in numerous congregations. This sermon was preached on March 17, 2013 (Lent 5C), as part of the March 2013 Gun Sabbath weekend.

For Reflection

1. Where is your story in this story?
2. Where do you see God?
3. What causes you to pause and rethink your previous assumptions?
4. What cries out to you?
5. What calls to you?

Go Deeper

1. What causes your "wills and affections" to become unruly?
2. When have you caught yourself "out of control"? What led to this realization and how did you (if you did) regain control?
3. When has something gone horribly wrong for you? What made it bearable, if anything? What helped you continue to go on?

Put Your Sword Back into Its Place

Mark Bozzuti-Jones

While he was still speaking, Judas, one of the twelve, arrived; with him was a large crowd with swords and clubs, from the chief priests and the elders of the people. Now the betrayer had given them a sign, saying, "The one I will kiss is the man; arrest him." At once he came up to Jesus and said, "Greetings, Rabbi!" and kissed him. Jesus said to him, "Friend, do what you are here to do." Then they came and laid hands on Jesus and arrested him. Suddenly, one of those with Jesus put his hand on his sword, drew it, and struck the slave of the high priest, cutting off his ear. Then Jesus said to him, "Put your sword back into its place; for all who take the sword will perish by the sword. Do you think that I cannot appeal to my Father, and he will at once send me more than twelve legions of angels? But how then would the scriptures be fulfilled, which say it must happen in this way?" At that hour Jesus said to the crowds, "Have you come out with swords and clubs to arrest me as though I were a bandit? Day after day I sat in the temple teaching, and you did not arrest me. But all this has taken place, so that the scriptures of

*the prophets may be fulfilled." Then all the disciples
deserted him and fled.* (Matthew 26:47–56)

"Put your sword back into its place; for all who take the sword will
perish by the sword."

Every so often, we get a message that is loud and clear, unequivocal in its direction, from the lips of Jesus. When we hear such
a message, we know without doubt what Jesus thought, valued,
taught, and wished. Put your sword back into its place. Put your
sword away. Do not use your sword. Do not use your sword to
defend yourself. Do not use your sword to defend me. Do not use
your sword to save your own life and do not use your sword to
defend mine.

I read somewhere that a research commissioned by Congress
shows that there are over 310 million firearms in the United States.
These firearms, not owned by the military or government officials, live in the homes of citizens like you and me. Imagine that,
think for a moment, over 310 million firearms. In 2012, there were
close to 9,000 deaths by firearms, with close to 7,000 attributed to
handguns. What is even more disturbing is that 61 percent of all
gun-related deaths are from suicide.

Put your sword back into its place.

The issue of violence, death, and suffering committed by us in
what purports to be a Christian nation is a scandal that the gospel
calls us to face. The nature of God, the Prince of Peace, challenges
us to redefine what it means to be a people of God and a people
who embrace the name of God. Put your sword back into its place
becomes the twenty-first-century call to discipleship. This new call
to discipleship goes out to the whole world.

My dear brothers and sisters, would to God that this nation
that calls itself a Christian nation would listen to the words of
Jesus. We need to put our guns away and put them away for good
and cause no harm with them. Ten thousand people are shot
every year in America. Since the 2012 shooting in Sandy Hook
Elementary School in Connecticut, there have been approximately
fifty school shootings. Do you know that Americans make up only
4.5 percent of the world's population and own 40 percent of all
civilian guns? What kind of a Christian country is this? What does
it mean for a country that professes to be like Christ not to listen
to a very clear directive that comes from Christ to put the gun
away?

Our Gospel passage shows Jesus in one of his most vulnerable
encounters. He is afraid, knows his suffering and death are close

at hand, and he is struggling with what it means to be faithful to God's will.

We meet Jesus in today's Gospel speaking to his disciples. As he speaks, a crowd approaches him and the crowd includes one of his disciples. I invite you to meditate on these words for a brief moment. I will read a few verses, and I invite you to listen to them and allow them to invade your heart, soul, and mind.

> *Judas, one of the twelve, arrived; with him was a large crowd with swords and clubs, from the chief priests and the elders of the people. Now the betrayer had given them a sign, saying, "The one I will kiss is the man; arrest him." At once he came up to Jesus and said, "Greetings, Rabbi!" and kissed him. Jesus said to him, "Friend, do what you are here to do." Then they came and laid hands on Jesus and arrested him.* (Matthew 26:47–50)

Who are you in this drama? Are you Judas? Are you a member of the large crowd with swords and clubs? Are you Peter who pulls his sword to defend Jesus? Are you Jesus?

Our Gospel reading invites us to examine our role in the drama of Jesus's life and the drama of the world in which we live. At any one moment, we could be Judas, one of the twelve, who has allowed the wrong agenda to take root in his heart, soul, and mind. As we approach Jesus, what is in our heart? Who or what accompanies us?

Are You Judas?

It seems to me that in light of all this conversation about gun violence, we are indeed Judas. Notice, Judas is making his way toward Jesus; he is going to Jesus. However, his intentions are not good, his reason for going to Jesus is not in pursuit of what is good, true, and beautiful. I believe that Judas is America today. We are journeying toward Jesus with the wrong intentions. We are journeying toward Jesus with a crowd bearing swords and clubs. We the Christian nation, we the Christian Church, we the Christian are making our way toward Jesus with swords and clubs.

Dear friends, I hate to break it to you, but our journey toward Jesus will not lead to what is good, true, and beautiful if we make that journey accompanied by violence—with weapon in hand.

Are You the Crowd?

There was a large crowd with Judas. The Scripture described them as journeying toward Jesus with swords and clubs. In the recent debates, the money and lobbyists from the NRA have often spoken the loudest. They insist that part of being America and Americans requires that we bear arms and always have the freedom to bear arms. Many even advocate the right and freedom to bear arms in churches and schools.

The Gospel reading invites us to see the violence and chaos on the way to meet the solitude and peace of Jesus. The fact that the crowd felt the need to be brandishing and bearing their swords and clubs stands in stark contrast to Jesus the Prince of Peace.

I believe we are called to use this image of the crowd facing Jesus with their swords and clubs as a way of entering into this debate about the place and role of guns in our society. Why do we arm ourselves? What reasons do we believe that we need guns in our homes? Why do we feel the need to hunt and kill animals? As the story develops, there is no further mention of the crowds using their weapons. I think this is the Gospel's implicit invitation for us to put away our swords and clubs.

The crowd laid their hands on Jesus and arrested him. Wow. Dear friends in Christ, Jesus does not resist the intentions and actions of those who are evil. He is nonviolent in the face of violence. The history of violence shows that violence breeds violence, and Jesus shows the path of peace. In this encounter of Jesus and the armed crowd we are called to remember Gandhi, Martin Luther King Jr., and all the men and women who faced violence with nonviolence. As Jesus faced down this crowd, we are called to live the dream of God, where we do not return evil for evil, but face swords and clubs with a posture of nonviolence.

Unlike much of Scripture where the people of God defended themselves in battle, Jesus gives us a new paradigm. To most of us, in the face of violence and threats, the appropriate thing to do would be to arm ourselves, defend ourselves, and fight a just war. However, when we pay attention to the posture of Jesus, we see Jesus who calmly stands before the madding crowd. Jesus seems to draw near to them and calms them. It is clear from the Gospel reading that Jesus does not incite or fear them.

Jesus's encounter with the crowd invites us into a new experience of seeing and knowing Jesus as the one who desires peace. What would our lives as Christians look like if we stood up to violence with calm and confidence in God?

Are You One of Those with Jesus?

Tradition has oftentimes identified the disciple who "put his hand on his sword, drew it, and struck the slave of the high priest, cutting off his ear" as Peter. However, I like the fact that the Gospel reads "one of those with Jesus." It is noteworthy that the act of violence comes from the camp of Jesus, the flock of Jesus, one of those with Jesus.

In Matthew's Gospel, the theme of contrasts comes to its zenith in this passage. Imagine that—it is the Christian who causes the violence. In this simple act, the cutting off of the ear, we are called to reexamine our history of violence and our propensity to defend our arms. There is no justification for violence. Jesus does not condone shootings. Jesus does not condone inflicting pain in his name.

This reality that the crowd arrested Jesus without harm, while one of Jesus's followers causes harm should let the Church think about how easily it resorts to violence and condones violence. It will not surprise us that there are more wars fought in the name of God than we are willing to admit. Gun violence on an individual basis is weighed and found wanting: each of us must put away the sword. Gun violence on a national basis is weighed and found wanting: as a country we must stop producing arms. As children of God we are all weighed and found wanting—we must put our swords away.

Are You Jesus?

Matthew does not back away from inviting the individual to be like Jesus. Matthew boldly proclaims his Gospel as a call to be like Jesus and to see the fullness of Jesus in every human being. We remember the words: whatever you do to the least you do to me. Jesus embodies and identifies with the least and the vulnerable.

From this call to be like Jesus throughout the Gospel of Matthew we see the call for us to be like Jesus and face down violence without resorting to violence. We are called to be like Jesus and to be the one who proclaims put your sword away.

> Let the Spirit of God fill us with the courage to believe
> and know that we are in God's hands.
> Let the Spirit of God fill us with the grace and courage
> to be peacemakers.

Let the Spirit of God fill us with wisdom and strength to speak truth to power and put an end to violence in our country and world.
Let the Spirit of God lead us all to a new place of being brave enough to find in an imitation of Jesus the correct response to violence.

Yes, this is the good news and the hard news in Christ from our Gospel, not just today, but every day: when we journey toward Jesus with our swords, clubs, and guns, it will only lead to betrayal.

Jesus says to us loudly and clearly, put your sword back in its place, put your sword away, *you cannot journey toward me or with me with guns.*

Dear God, please help us to put an end to the killing in our land. Dear God, help us to put our guns away. Amen.

Lord, make me an instrument of Thy peace;
Where there is hatred, let me sow love;
Where there is injury, pardon;
Where there is error, the truth;
Where there is doubt, the faith;
Where there is despair, hope;
Where there is darkness, light;
And where there is sadness, joy.

O Divine Master,
Grant that I may not so much seek
To be consoled, as to console;
To be understood, as to understand;
To be loved as to love.

For it is in giving that we receive;
It is in pardoning that we are pardoned;
And it is in dying that we are born to eternal life. Amen.[22]

---

22   "A Prayer attributed to St. Francis," The Book of Common Prayer (New York: Church Publishing Incorporated, 1979), 833.

The Reverend Mark Bozzuti-Jones is a former Roman Catholic Jesuit priest and today is an Episcopal priest. He is a one-time missionary in Brazil, a forever Jamaican, and a lover of poetry, people, and the undisputed emperor of selfies. Mark is the director of pastoral care at Trinity Wall Street, New York City. A father of a seventh grader and the husband of Kathy, an interfaith minister, Mark believes wholeheartedly that we are children of God—all of us. This sermon was delivered on June 19, 2014.

For Reflection

1. Where is your story in this story?
2. Where do you see God?
3. What causes you to pause and rethink your previous assumptions?
4. What cries out to you?
5. What calls to you?

Go Deeper

1. Who are you in this drama? Are you Judas? Are you a member of the large crowd with swords and clubs? Are you Peter who pulls his sword to defend Jesus? Are you Jesus?
2. When have you been vulnerable? What has your response been?
3. What invitation is Jesus offering you?
4. What would your life as a Christian look like if you stood up to violence with calm and confidence in God?

11

The Way of Life and Peace: The Church's Advocacy against Violence

Alexander D. Baumgarten

> Almighty God, whose most dear Son went not up to joy but first he suffered pain, and entered not into glory before he was crucified: Mercifully grant that we, walking in the way of the cross, may find it none other than the way of life and peace; through Jesus Christ your Son our Lord, who lives and reigns with you and the Holy Spirit, one God, for ever and ever. Amen. (Book of Common Prayer, 220)

During Holy Week of 2013, on a snowy morning in Washington just months after the terrible violence at Sandy Hook Elementary School, I prayed the ancient Stations of the Cross with approximately twenty-five bishops and hundreds of Episcopalians from around the United States while walking from the White House to the Capitol. Led by the bishops of the Episcopal Diocese of Connecticut, the ritual offered a public liturgical commitment to addressing the culture of violence in America that led to so many unnecessary deaths not just in Newtown, Connecticut, but also in countless cities and communities across the United States in the months and years before and since.

The planners of the walk chose Holy Week for this solemn commemoration because the culture of violence in our nation is the precise same culture of violence that, some two millenniums earlier, brought Jesus to the streets of Jerusalem for the final walk of his life. But the intersection of the bloody drama of the cross and the bloody reality of unchecked violence in our nation and communities today is more than a coincidence or a convenient narrative for teaching and preaching. As a Christian, I cannot fully understand my obligation to challenge the world's fixation on violence without understanding the cross, and I cannot understand the cross without understanding our world's fateful fixation on violence.

The Way of the Cross in a World Scarred by Violence

As we walked that morning, I found myself meditating continually on the above collect appointed by the Book of Common Prayer for Monday in Holy Week. Penned by the Reverend William Reed Huntington, then-rector of Grace Church in Manhattan, for the 1892 American Prayer Book, the collect draws on two phrases—"went not up to joy but first he suffered pain" and "entered not into glory before he was crucified"—that originally appeared in the 1662 Prayer Book's rite for the visitation of the sick. Huntington, one of the great ecumenists of The Episcopal Church and a leader in the House of Deputies—he was a deputy for thirty-six years!—added the collect's petition himself: "Grant that we, walking the way of the cross, may find it none other than the way of life and peace."

The way of life and peace.

Walking the way of the cross on the snowy streets of Washington, as I have multiple times on the ancient (but seldom snowy) streets of Jerusalem where the Stations' devotion originated in an attempt to retrace the footsteps of Jesus on his final day, I wondered: What precisely about the way of the cross—a road, quite literally, stained with blood—makes it the way of life? What makes it the way of peace, of all things? How does violence and suffering draw Christians onto a road that leads to life and peace?

The Church's traditional interpretation, and indeed the precise meaning of the collect, is that our own earthly sufferings are holy because they draw us mystically into the sufferings of Jesus. "Suffering produces endurance," declares Paul in his letter to the Romans, "and endurance produces character, and character produces hope, and hope does not disappoint us, because God's love has been poured into our hearts through the Holy Spirit that has been given to us" (5:3–5).

While I identify spiritually with this interpretation in a profound way, I feel certain that in order to understand the senseless human suffering wrought by violence in our world today, and faithfully discern how God calls us to respond, we must adopt a much broader understanding of the cross. Surely we are not to tell those who have lost loved ones as a result of unfettered societal violence that their sufferings are holy. Surely we must reckon the mystery of the cross not simply as a call to perpetual suffering but rather as a vehicle for transformation.

The word "atonement," a traditional theme associated with the cross, gets a bad name amongst many modern Christians, perhaps because it reminds them of a theology steeped in wrath and punishment for sin rather than resurrection and redemption through baptism. However, the original meaning of the word, indeed its literal etymology in English, is deeply liberating and transformational. Atonement refers to the oneness of humanity with God ("at-one-ment") achieved by Jesus on the cross. The astounding miracle of the cross, the reason the cross becomes for Christians the fulcrum of all human history, is that through the sacrifice of Christ, God removes, in one fell swoop, all of the previously impermeable barriers separating humanity from the Divine. Because of the cross, God draws the whole human race into perfect oneness with God. As a great Episcopal priest who has now gone on to his own heavenly reward put it in a Good Friday sermon I will always remember: "As a consequence of the cross, when God now looks upon the world, he no longer sees sin and brokenness, but only the face of his Son." Here are the seeds of understanding the way of the cross as the way of life and peace.

Paul writes in his second letter to the Corinthians that "if anyone is in Christ, there is a new creation; everything old has passed away; See, everything has become new! All this is from God, who reconciled us to himself through Christ." Paul does not stop there, however. He adds that in this act of reconciliation God "has given us the ministry of reconciliation" (2 Corinthians 5: 17–18). In spite of God's cosmic and definitive redemption of the world, our temporary state of sin and brokenness still produces astounding levels of suffering and ungodliness in the world around us, and so God calls us through the cross to become agents of reconciliation in the world around us.

In the cross, we have seen the picture of what a reconciled world looks like, indeed how the world looks to God, and so our role is to labor to make the world look this way in the eyes of all the world's inhabitants today. The ghastly consequences of humanity's capacity for inhumanity—whether lived out in suburban schools, waves of urban crime, or in war zones many thousand miles away—must be to Christians intolerable affronts to the cross that goad us to press the world toward a different way. To live a life that challenges the world to replace the world's images of brokenness, suffering, violence, and injustice with the image of life and peace reflected in God's own beloved Son, is to walk the way of the cross.

Advocacy within the Charism of the Baptized and the Mission of God

This is the facet of the cross that envelops me every day as I lead the advocacy office of the Episcopal Church alongside the staff of the Domestic and Foreign Missionary Society (DFMS) who work to equip advocacy by Episcopalians throughout the church.[23] I get asked all the time by Episcopalians what it's like to be the "church's lobbyist" in Washington (sometimes with bemusement and sometimes with implicit indictment of why the church needs a lobbyist in Washington in the first place). I normally respond that this is not how I understand the work of the church's Office of Justice and Advocacy Ministries. In some cases, yes, our staff works with policymakers in Washington on behalf of the wider Church in pursuit of the various positions on social justice and peace that the General Convention deduces from the Scriptures, reason, and tradition. But our fundamental work—indeed the fundamental work of all of The Missionary Society, the churchwide staff—is to serve Episcopalians by providing the tools, and supporting the networks of individual Christians, that allow every Episcopalian to live into a ministry that is, in fact, the charism of all the baptized and an integral part of the mission of God.

Advocacy is the charism of all the baptized because advocacy is, in so many cases, the surest and the quickest means by which to effect the transformation of the world that is the way of the cross. Our prayer book, of course, underscores this in the baptismal rite

---

23 The Domestic and Foreign Missionary Society is the name under which the Episcopal Church is incorporated. The churchwide staff of the Episcopal Church commonly is referred to as the staff of The Missionary Society.

itself by pressing the candidate to promise not just to "strive for justice and peace among all people," but also to "seek and serve Christ in all persons" and "proclaim by word and example the Good News of God in Christ."[24]

I understand these words and promises to have both an individual component, a pledge to seek right relationships that reflect justice and peace in my own daily life, and a community and even cosmic component. Even if every small sphere of my life and my relationships is steeped in perfect justice, peace, and right relationship, I am falling short of what God asks of me if I can be at peace with a world in which this is not the case for all. Far from being a "political" distraction from the work of the gospel, the pursuit of a world transformed from its own sinful and violent disfigurement is a component of the total gospel that concerns itself with both the souls and the bodies of God's people. Archbishop Desmond Tutu puts it memorably when he says:

> I don't preach a social gospel, I preach *the* Gospel, period.
> The Gospel of Our Lord Jesus Christ is concerned for
> the whole person. When people were hungry, Jesus didn't
> say, "Now is this political or social?" He said, "I feed you,"
> because the good news to a hungry person is bread.[25]

We might easily add that to a person beset by violence all around him, or a person who sees her community and family unraveled daily by conflict and strife, the good news—the gospel—is peace. A society that continually besieges the bodies of its people with violence cannot possibly produce a collective soul that is in union with God.

As surely as advocacy is one charism of the baptized (and indeed because it is), it is also one integral component of the mission of God and the mission of the Church. The Prayer Book's catechism, mirroring Paul's summation of the gospel as the ministry of reconciliation, tells us that the "mission of the Church is to restore all people to unity with God and each other in Christ." It then goes on to say that the Church lives out this mission as it "prays and worships, proclaims the Gospel, and promotes justice, peace, and love."[26] This last summation holds a key to the rest because,

---

24   The 1979 Book of Common Prayer, 305.

25   Harold T. Lewis, *A Church for the Future: South Africa as the Crucible for Anglicanism in a New Century* (New York: Church Publishing, 2007), 65.

26   BCP, 855.

correctly understood, it reminds us that each of the three acts it describes—spiritual discipline and communion with God, evangelism and telling of the Good News, and the pursuit of a world transformed from its own brokenness—are facets of the same jewel: mission. When one of those facets is missing or disfigured, the entire jewel is fractured and stripped of its brilliance.

As with the word "atonement," the word "mission" (and its derivative description of a human being, *missionary*) can draw negative, but ultimately unfair, characterizations in many modern Christian circles. Presumably this is because of concern about historical practices of missionaries who sought to subjugate or blunt local cultures. However, like the word "atonement," the words "mission" and "missionary" convey something not only integral, but quite liberating and revolutionary about the community of Jesus Christ, and the Church discards them at its own peril.

To be a missionary is to be one who is *sent*, and sent for a particular purpose. Just as some call the Eucharist "the Mass" after its final words in Latin, *Ite Missa Est*—"Go, you are sent"—in order to underscore that the transcendent mystery of the Blessed Sacrament is not to be hidden in the bushel that is the church building but rather taken to the streets through the ministry of reconciliation, so too is the Church's total identity incomprehensible if it does not involve sending Christians into the world to seek the transformation of souls and bodies. The word "mission," like the dismissal at the end of the Eucharist, has always reminded me of the story of the Transfiguration, in which a wide-eyed Peter suggests aloud—in a near-nonsensical and wishful babble—that the disciples and Jesus remain on the mountaintop permanently, gazing in awe at Jesus revealed by the Father, at long last, to be what he truly is (Matthew 17: 1-9). "Let us sit here," it is as if he says, "and luxuriate in this moment of transformation." But Jesus swiftly rebukes him and bids the disciples to come down from the mountaintop, because the transformation of the disciples is useless unless they are sent into the world to serve as witnesses to transformation.

This is what it is to be a missionary; this is why the act of being sent in mission is the fundamental marker of Christian discipleship. When considered this way, advocacy for social changes that reflect the world as it looks in God's eyes become quite obviously an integral component of being sent into the world. If mission has been lived out sinfully in the past, the response of Christians today must be to live it out as Jesus willed it in sending his disciples down from the mountain. The point is not, of course, to subjugate other cultural expressions, but to transform the ways of the world—violence, hunger, poverty, and injustice—that inhibit the reconciliation of bodies and souls. I am a missionary because my own transformation in Christ is meaningless, indeed it is folly, if I am at peace with a world in which others suffer.

Does Our Advocacy Make a Difference?

Advocacy—no matter how grounded in mission or the gospel—is still useless unless it actually produces change. Would those of us who lack the power to command armies or write national budgets not be better off using our time on classic acts of Christian charity: feeding the hungry or visiting the sick in our own backyard? Such acts clearly affect transformation, even if it is on an individual scale, while time spent writing to a lawmaker or leading a community meeting might seem more obtuse. The welcome news is that if impact is one's guiding principle, one need not choose between acts of charity and acts of justice-through-advocacy because the impact of both is clear.

Here are four areas in which the advocacy of Christians—specifically the organized, collective advocacy witness of The Episcopal Church—has helped, or is helping to, transform society. The first involves a global debate, the second a national debate, the third a state debate, and the fourth a local emergency:

1.   **The Jubilee 2000 Movement for Global Economic Justice**. The late 1990s worldwide campaign for global debt cancellation and economic justice germinated in faith communities and produced tangible global and American policies that directly led to millions of children in poor countries attending school when they otherwise would not have, millions of people living lives free of HIV or malaria, and millions of Africans and others in the developing world having electricity and running water. The then-presiding bishop of The Episcopal Church was the first faith leader to testify to the United States Congress about the Jubilee movement in the 1990s,[27] the worldwide 1998 Lambeth conference of Anglican bishops produced a significant statement on the topic,[28] and countless Episcopalians became involved in Jubilee advocacy in their own local contexts. Representative Nancy Pelosi, who would later become the first female Speaker

---

27   http://archive.wfn.org/1999/07/msg00059.html.
28   http://www.lambethconference.org/resolutions/1998/1998-1-15.cfm.

of the House, has described the Jubilee 2000 movement led by faith groups as the single-most effective movement for social justice that she's witnessed.[29] (The Rt. Reverend M. Thomas Shaw wrote in detail about the role of Episcopalians in this work in his book *Conversations with Scripture and Each Other*.[30])

2. **The Preservation of Alaska's Arctic National Wildlife Refuge from Drilling**. Since the late 1970s, American policymakers have debated the question of whether the coastal plain of Alaska should be opened to oil exploration and drilling, with drilling advocates gaining new momentum in the early 2000s as oil prices skyrocketed and Americans increasingly became concerned about energy independence. The Episcopal Church's witness in opposition to drilling grew out of the experiences and perspectives of the Gwich'in, the northernmost Indian nation in the world, who live in the Refuge and are, because of nineteenth-century missionary history, 93 percent Episcopal. The Gwich'in, whose name means "people of the land" subsist on the Porcupine Caribou, a species that would be threatened by drilling, for 60–70 percent of their diet, for clothing, and for many aspects of their culture. Through the combined efforts of the bishop of Alaska, the Gwich'in Steering Committee, the church's Office of Justice and Advocacy Ministries, and thousands of people in the pews, the Episcopal Church became the most active U.S.-based denomination working to fight off congressional and administration efforts to drill. Despite the U.S. president and the majority leadership in both houses of congress supporting drilling in the early 2000s, Episcopalians mounted a substantial and successful grassroots campaign, sustained over many years, to preserve the sanctity of the land. Public-policy advocacy was accompanied by economic advocacy, as Episcopal leaders and staff worked with the Church of England, a major shareholder in British Petroleum, to successfully prevent BP from lending its influential voice to the cause of drilling.[31] After more than a decade of congressional debate, pro drilling forces still have not been successful in winning authorization for widespread drilling.

3. **The Abolition of Capital Punishment in Connecticut in 2012**. The bishops, clergy, and people of the Diocese of Connecticut—including a State Public Policy Network working with the Missionary Society's churchwide Office of Justice and

---

29   In 2007 meeting with the author.
30   Published by Rowan and Littlefield, 2007.
31   http://archive.episcopalchurch.org/3577_36702_ENG_HTM.htm.

Advocacy Ministries—led a concerted campaign of teaching, public witness, legislative advocacy, and prayer that helped make Connecticut the seventeenth state overall, and the fifth in five years, to abolish capital punishment. The Episcopal Church's General Convention of 1958 voiced opposition to the death penalty, and this has been the collective witness of the church ever since. The Connecticut campaign[32] provided many excellent examples of the Church applying a longstanding social witness of the Convention to an emergent movement in a particular state context, collaborating with ecumenical, interfaith, and secular partners.

4. **Reconciliation in an American Community Scarred by Violence**. In August 2014, when police in Ferguson, Missouri, shot an unarmed African-American teenager after an incident whose details still remain unclear, the community responded with widespread protest. As some in the community turned to further violence and looting in the aftermath of the incident, and local police and state officials responded in ways that generated significant public controversy, national debate in the United States focused extensively, but ultimately briefly, on underlying dynamics of racial relations, violence, and poverty in American communities. Episcopal churches in Ferguson and elsewhere in the greater St. Louis area, along with the bishop of Missouri, began working daily with churchwide staff to provide immediate material relief in the wake of community upheaval, teaching and spiritual formation about the underlying issues of tension, advocacy for policies to respond to the brokenness, and initiatives for healing and reconciliation after the news cameras left. In the immediate aftermath of the events in Ferguson, Bishop Stacy F. Sauls, chief operating officer of The Episcopal Church, announced a $30,000 grant of The Missionary Society to the Diocese of Missouri, which was then complemented by $10,000 from Episcopal Relief & Development, for an innovative partnership of the diocese and parishes in working toward reconciliation and restoration. The initiative focused on the provision of food and other immediate needs, the development of a community collaborative for economic revitalization and recovery, and the initiation of a public/private partnership to involve the community's young in the meeting of human need. Such a response might be thought of as advocacy through

---

32   http://episcopaldigitalnetwork.com/ens/2012/06/13/episcopal-leaders-push-to-abolish-death-penalty-across-the-country/#comments.

witness. At the time I write this, these initiatives are brand new; I pray that by the time my words appear in print, the fruits of this labor will be well-known and documented.

These are but four examples. Given limitless space, one could discuss countless other successes, including the Church's historical role in the American civil rights movement and the global campaign to end apartheid in South Africa; the successful advocacy of Episcopalians in the late 1990s to create a congressionally chartered independent U.S. commission for the protection of religious liberty around the world; the astoundingly effective ongoing work of Episcopalians against the violence of human trafficking in a variety of local contexts; and the creative ways in which Episcopalians and Anglicans in a number of nations are working to combat gender violence.

The Path Forward on Gun Violence

If each of the above examples provides some hope and inspiration, the troubling persistence (and indeed continued rise) of seemingly endless gun violence in American communities should deeply unsettle us. The advocacy of Episcopalians and other people of faith has not lacked; it simply has yet to fully bear its intended fruit.

Presiding Bishop Katharine Jefferts Schori in early 2013 provided testimony to the United States Senate on how Americans might come together to create comprehensive and consensus-based responses to violence that transcend the polarities of "gun control" versus "gun rights."[33] Thousands of grassroots Episcopalians have involved themselves in working toward the transformation outlined by the presiding bishop, but—as was the case after the shooting and violence in Ferguson—national attention proved fleeting and public debate, as well as government officials, seemed quickly to move on to the next crisis. Far from discouraging us, this should provide us with the inspiration to press forward as voices in the wilderness.

However, the church's advocacy continues in full measure, authentically grounded in communities of presence, even when the attention of society at large has moved to other subjects. Just as the church does not stop walking the way of the cross when Holy

---

33 http://www.episcopalchurch.org/notice/episcopal-presiding-bishop-provides-testimony-gun-violence-senate-judiciary-subcommittee.

Week ends—a fact in which the Prayer Book reminds us by giving us Huntington's beautiful collect not just at the outset of Holy Week but in the Office of Morning Prayer every single Friday—neither does the Church's charism of advocacy for justice and peace cease when the attention of the world turns elsewhere.

This persistence is more than faithful discipleship, a sort of noble and quixotic adherence to principle even when it seems foolish; it is, at its core, the hallmark of truly effective and truly transformative advocacy. The historian and reporter Richard Kluger, in his seminal volume on the American civil rights movement, *Simple Justice*, writes at length about the degree to which *Brown v. Board of Education* and all that followed was rooted in decades of concerted and physically and spiritually costly strategic advocacy—much of it born in American churches—that is now mostly forgotten in the public imagination. Without it, though, *Brown* likely would never have happened, or would have happened very differently and perhaps much later. Change does not happen in a vacuum, and it rarely is the product of emotions stirred in the wake of a crisis. Rather, it is born of dogged persistence no matter what the level of engagement by the wider world.

The tragedy, of course, is those who must suffer in the time before change comes. How many millions of people suffered waiting for *Brown* (and have suffered waiting for the full realization of its promise, even today)? How many have lost their lives, and will lose their lives, because public appetite for a debate on gun violence seems to ebb as soon as the next crisis comes?

This question should inspire us to press forward. And it should remind us of the most basic understanding of the cross of Jesus Christ: that because the cross involves God entering physically and personally into the reality of human suffering, it is capacious enough to hold all such sufferings and, eventually, to make the broken whole again:

> O mysterious condescending!
> O abandonment sublime!
> Very God himself is bearing
> All the sufferings of time![34]

---

34 William J. Sparrow-Simpson, "Cross of Jesus, Cross of Sorrow," *The Hymnal* (New York: Church Pension Fund, 1985), 160.

Alexander D. Baumgarten is director of Justice and Advocacy Ministries for The Episcopal Church, advising the presiding bishop and leading a staff team that works to equip Episcopalians for the work of justice and peacemaking. He lives in Alexandria, Virginia, and is a member of St. Paul's Church, K Street, in Washington.

For Reflection

1. Where is your story in this story?
2. Where do you see God?
3. What causes you to pause and rethink your previous assumptions?
4. What cries out to you?
5. What calls to you?

Go Deeper

1. What does advocacy mean to you?
2. How have you been an advocate for someone else?
3. What do you believe the role of the Church and its members has in advocating for peace and justice in the public sector?
4. What charism do you (or your community) have for advocacy that has yet to be acted upon?

12

Swords into Plowshares and Arms into Art: A Practical Theology of Transformation and Witness

James E. Curry

The theology of "Reclaiming the Gospel of Peace" begins with the person of Jesus and God's action of love, blessing, and transformation on the cross.

Jesus said: "Blessed are the peacemakers, for they will be called children of God." In the face of the epidemic of gun violence in our society, many of us are motivated by our faith in Jesus, and yet we feel we lack the tools and the imagination to be peacemakers. What can we say or do that can interpret our faith in the Gospel of Peace and lead to actions that truly effect change?

As Christians I think we have a toolkit of resources that is both obvious and underutilized. We are people of prayer, faith, Scripture, and symbol. We know that God's own mission is ultimately a peace-building mission of reconciliation and restoration. Jesus himself is our peace and the one who puts us on the mission path to be peacemakers.

There are no easy solutions to the scourge of gun violence in our cities and towns. As we begin to work in our communities to challenge violence and as we continue to build alliances with other peace-seeking organizations, we will continue to run into political obstacles, apathy, and hostility. Grounded in our faith, we can point to what God has done already to transform the world and we can follow Jesus who faced the violence of his culture in prayer and action. In his death and resurrection we find life.

The Gospel of Peace calls us to public witness grounded in prayer. In 2012, as the Connecticut House and Senate were debating a ban on the death penalty in this state, the bishops of Connecticut invited clergy of our church and other denominations to join us out on the streets of Hartford to pray the Stations of the Cross with special intention for the welfare of our communities and for the abolition of the death penalty. As over one hundred and eighty clergy and laypeople processed out from Christ Church Cathedral through downtown Hartford, we prayed for the victims of violence and for perpetrators of violence. We prayed for civic leaders and the people of all of our communities. We prayed for the poor and the homeless, and also for decision makers and people in positions of authority. We prayed for children and teachers, for peace in our homes, hope on our streets, and the courage to work for justice in our society. At each Station of the Cross, we made a connection between Jesus's journey through Jerusalem on the last day of his life and the work of God's mission of restoration and reconciliation in our own state and our own capital city.

When I was consecrated as bishop suffragan of the Episcopal Church in Connecticut, I was given a beautiful gold bejeweled cross on a matching gold chain. I do not wear that cross very often anymore. It has become for me both too beautiful and too precious. I truly believe in the power of symbols and that beautiful cross seems too far removed from the reality of Jesus's sacrifice and the power of God's love to recreate the world.

The pectoral cross I do wear was a gift from the Anglican Diocese of Lebombo in Mozambique. It is made from pieces of destroyed weapons that had been used in their devastating civil war. The upright of this cross is the piston of the automatic action of an AK-47 (the key component of a gun whose only purpose is to kill). The arms of the cross are made from the sight mounts of the AK-47. The cross is big, heavy, and far from pretty. It is also the most powerful symbol and instrument I have to preach the Gospel of Peace. (See page 39.)

Whenever I wear this cross people ask me about it. And each time I have the opportunity to tell the story of the transformation of one country and the hope that we also might be able to affect change in our society through deep faith and action in the Gospel of Peace.

Mozambique is a poor country on the southeastern coast of Africa. Until 1975 it was a colony of Portugal. At the time of its independence, neighboring Rhodesia (ruled by a white minority) and Apartheid South Africa fomented a guerrilla movement in Mozambique because they feared a strong black majority, socialist neighbor. Mozambique, which had no arms industry of its own, was flooded with weapons. The civil war went on for seventeen years. During the war every infrastructure of the country was destroyed: roads and railroads, the electrical and communications grid, education, and health care.

Throughout the years of war, the Anglican Church continued to fast and pray and work for peace. Their bishop, Dinis Sengulane, sought out the leaders of the warring factions, imploring them to join in peace talks. The church never gave up praying and seeking peace. Over and over again Bishop Sengulane would bring the message of the Gospel of Peace to leaders of the government and leaders of the opposition. His message was constant: blessed are the peacemakers for they shall be called children of God. Year after year the church was thwarted in its efforts. Until in one meeting there was a breakthrough and the leader of the opposition party said to Bishop Sengulane, "All these years you have been saying the same thing to me. Now I understand, we must come to peace."

The Anglican Church's experience in Mozambique is a reminder to us to stay focused in prayer as we seek to challenge violence in our own communities. Prayer and fasting are the Christian foundation for work over the long haul.

Following a ceasefire in 1992, Bishop Sengulane and the Anglican Church lead a campaign to rid the countryside of the guns that were being stockpiled in homes and villages. The Christian Council of Mozambique mounted an exchange program to give tools for guns. Anyone who brought in a gun or ammunition to be destroyed was given an instrument of production for their life beyond war: tools for subsistence farming, simple building materials for repairing homes, bicycles, and peddle sewing machines. Bishop Sengulane led the campaign with the message: "Having a gun in your house is like having a poisonous snake in your home; eventually it will bite you or someone you love." Members of the church took that message into every village and the people responded.

Every weapon that was turned in was destroyed on site—never to be able to be used again to harm someone. Most of the guns were sawn into pieces. Over the last twenty-two years, nearly a million weapons have been destroyed and Mozambique has not gone back into war.

The persistent proclamation of the Gospel of Peace fundamentally changed how the culture of the country of Mozambique understood itself. Many of the underlying social issues of the country still persist. Food and water security as well as issues of educational and economic development still plague Mozambican society, but armed conflict and armed street violence have been minimized to be almost nonexistent.

As guns were being collected and destroyed, Bishop Sengulane challenged the artists of Mozambique to use the pieces of weapons to make objects of art that show hope and embody the message of transformation.

The signature piece of the work of these artists is the Tree of Life now on permanent display in the British Museum.[35] Artists from the collective, Núcleo de Arte, created a fourteen-foot-tall metal tree from destroyed weapons. As one looks at the trunk that rises from the ground, it is obvious that it is formed from welded metal—recognizable pieces of guns. The branches are the barrels of rifles, and the leaves are ammunition magazines of automatic weapons. Whimsical animals, also made from destroyed weapons, climb in its branches and play on the ground in its shade.

When the Tree of Life was first displayed on the streets of Maputo, the capital of Mozambique, people were encouraged to write, in a guestbook, their own pledge not to use guns or other weapons of war. What began as a challenge from the church to give substance to the proclamation of the Gospel of Peace has become an international movement of artists and citizens. Members of Núcleo de Arte have also created a Throne of Weapons, which is at the Vatican Museum, pieces of art displayed around the world, and the simple cross that I wear.

People stop me every day to ask about the cross I wear. And as soon as I say that it is made from destroyed weapons, they get it. Even non-Christians understand the symbol of a cross that is made from destroyed guns that had once been used to kill people in war.

Every Sunday I ask the children of the parish where I am visiting to join me for the Blessing at the close of Holy Eucharist. We gather in front of the altar and talk about what a blessing is. The children range from preschoolers to late teens and our conversation sometimes goes far afield. Usually we come back to my definition of a blessing: a laser beam of God's love given to each of us. I talk about how I, as bishop, am always asked to give a blessing at the

---

35 https://www.britishmuseum.org/explore/online_tours/museum_and_exhibition/
audio_description_tour/tree_of_life.aspx.

end of the service. And I invite them to help me in giving God's blessing to everyone in church by making the sign of the cross.

Before we join in Blessing, I ask, "Why would the sign of the cross be a sign of God's blessing?" Always one of the children shouts out, "Because Jesus died on the cross."

Indeed that is the blessing of the cross. Jesus loved us so much that he died on the cross for us. Jesus confronted the violence of the world and in the power of his love changed forever an instrument of death and humiliation into the symbol of our greatest hope.

I then tell the children (and, of course, everyone else in the congregation) the story of the cross I wear—that guns that had been used to hurt and kill people were destroyed so that no one could ever be hurt by them again. I pass around the cross and explain that the destroyed guns were reshaped by artists to become a sign of blessing. And, I tell them, that in the action of Jesus dying on the cross, God has taken the worst we can do to one another, i.e., kill and torture each other, and in Jesus's great love for the whole world has destroyed the old meaning of the cross and has reshaped the cross to be the symbol of hope and new life. Then, together, we make the sign of the cross over the people and say the words of blessing.

We are people reshaped by Jesus's great love for us. The Gospel of Peace is the proclamation of God's radical transformation of human tendencies toward violence into the new possibility of reconciliation. We have symbols to share and stories to tell.

And, of course, we are not alone in our desire to affect positive change in our communities. Our message builds on and dovetails with many other community organizations.

In September 2014, California artist Michael Kalish was invited by the city council and police department of Hartford, Connecticut, to install a sculpture made from two thousand pounds of confiscated and destroyed illegal guns in the park in front of the Connecticut State Capitol. It is a large framed sculpture of two people clasping hands.[36]

This is the first large piece of public art created from destroyed weapons that has been displayed in Hartford. Its beauty, size, and placement in Bushnell Park in the center of the city have given the people of Hartford a focal point for community conversation. After five months in Hartford, the sculpture will travel to Detroit and other cities.

Like most communities, Hartford struggles with the effects of gun violence and is seeking ways to encourage community conversation

---

36   See p. 179.

and action. Michael Kalish, like the artists of Mozambique, has transformed weapons of violence into a statement of hope and new possibility. The transformation that happens when recognizable pieces of weapons are turned into art can fuel proclamation, discussion, and prophetic witness.

Such works of art remind us of the sheer magnitude of the number of guns in our country. Confiscation of illegal guns and police buyback programs of weapons are positive programs that are beginning to have effect in many communities. Police departments are ready allies for groups who want to get guns off the street. Churches and local artists can certainly work with local police departments in developing their own creative symbols of transformation in the art of recycled weapons.

Police departments are rightly careful about what happens with confiscated or exchanged weapons. They want to make sure that the guns cannot be repurposed as weapons on the street. In some communities, the metal of weapons has been melted down and refabricated into art. In other communities church leaders and artists have encouraged police to destroy weapons in such a way that they cannot be reused for violence, but can be recognizable components of transformed art. There are endless possibilities for coalitions of artists and community leaders that can nurture art itself and foster the creative envisioning of communities transformed. Master classes in high school and college art programs, led by sculptors like Michael Kalish, can feed the imagination, give new possibility for creative expression among teenagers and young adults, and continue to raise the visibility of options to gun violence.

The Right Reverend James E. Curry is convener of Bishops Working for a Just World[37] and is a retired bishop suffragan of the Episcopal Church in Connecticut. He works with faith communities

---

37 Bishops Working for a Just World is a caucus within the House of Bishops devoted to fulfilling the Baptismal Covenant to "strive for justice and peace and respect the dignity of every human being." Organized by the Episcopal Public Policy's Office of Government Relations, the seven bishops, guided by General Convention resolutions, lobby Congress and meet with elected officials and/or their staffs on behalf of the Episcopal Church.

and secular organizations to create public witness to challenge violence through liturgy, the arts, and legislative advocacy.

For Reflection

1. Where is your story in this story?
2. Where do you see God?
3. What causes you to pause and rethink your previous assumptions?
4. What cries out to you?
5. What calls to you?

Go Deeper

1. Do you wear a cross? What does it represent to you and what story does it tell?
2. What signs of blessings can you bestow on others?
3. What symbols do you have to share and what stories to tell?
4. How might you partner with local law enforcement and artists to transform weapons of violence into images of hope in your community?

Your Hand in Mine

Roger Hutchison

I will never forget his face. Or his hands.

The young boy with dark eyes and small brown hands crouched under the table frantically trying to get away from something I could not see. He did not look at me. He looked through me. His eyes were wet with tears and ripe with anxiety—certainly witness to more than his share of pain.

I was in the midst of leading a "Painting Table" session with the children of the Episcopal Diocese of Upper South Carolina's Gravatt Camp and Conference Center's Reach Out Camp. Reach Out Camp (ROC) is a special session offered free of charge to children in first through eighth grade with one or more parent incarcerated.

The design of a Painting Table session is simple. People of any age are invited to gather around a table and create a painting using their fingers, acrylic paints, and paper or canvas. The end result of the Painting Table is not the painting that is created. It is the conversation, sharing, and listening that takes place among the people at the table. While there is grief, sadness, and loss, there is also hope.

The camp staff felt that the sixty children attending this week of camp would enjoy—and hopefully benefit—from this painting exercise.

As the children began to paint, I saw a young boy clutch his paper and dive under the table. His counselor tried to coax him back out, but he had retreated to a place deep within his mind and wounded soul. Hiding under the table was where he needed to be. His small hands were frantically ripping the paper into small shreds; a small pile of "I surrender" building at his feet.

The staff did a beautiful job of making sure he was safe. They gave him more paper to tear and a glass of water.

He was safe; maybe for the first time in his young life.

I sat down on the floor next to him and asked him his name.

No response.

I reached out my hand, palm-side up, inviting him to put his hand in mind. I wanted him to know that I cared. My hand remained empty and he continued to shred paper under the shelter of the table. "Would you like to paint a picture?" I asked him.

He shook his head no.

"May I sit with you for a time?"

He nodded a very slight yes.

The room was filled with the jubilant hymn of children's voices. Children were laughing, telling stories, and sharing their dreams. These same children whose lives have been shattered by gun violence, gang activity, and absolute desperation were spreading the colors of hope and joy in an otherwise colorless and frightening world. These are the same children whose parent or parents are not home to tuck them in at night because they are behind bars.

The young boy under the table seemed to settle down a bit. The demons that sent him scampering away in fear had retreated and the light was returning to his eyes. I caught him glancing over my way—looking at my paint-covered hands.

"Would you like to paint now? I am happy to get another sheet of paper for you, or, how about we paint on the newsprint that covers the table? I would enjoy painting with you."

Much to my surprise, the young boy moved from underneath the table and took a seat next to me. There were no other children at the table—it was just me, the boy, and his young college-aged counselor trying earnestly to get him to reconnect to the others in the room.

I sensed that the boy was not quite ready to put his fingers in the paint. We waited and looked around the room. In that brief moment, I saw a transformed dining hall full of altars draped with the finest of linen instead of picnic tables covered in paint-covered newsprint. I saw a sanctuary filled with children gathered around those altars—laughing, loving, and healing. Their young lives transformed by invitation and welcome to the holiest of tables where peace and joy reigns supreme.

I placed my hand into the red paint, spread my fingers wide, and placed it squarely on the newsprint that covered the table. He looked at me, then back at the paint on the table. He placed his hand in the paint, opened his fingers wide, and *made his mark* on the paper next to mine. He did it again and again. This same little boy who never shared his voice with me and took refuge under the table found his place at the table.

As our morning together came to a close, he dipped his small hand into the paint once more, opened his fingers wide, and placed his hand over my handprint. He looked up at me and smiled.

The image of his small hand in mine on the newsprint and forever etched on my heart is something I will never forget.

Roger Hutchison is the canon for children's ministries at Trinity Cathedral in Columbia, South Carolina. An artist, his first book, *The Painting Table: A Journal of Loss and Joy* (New York: Morehouse, 2014) has been used by people of all ages in schools, churches, and community groups across the United States, including the children of Trinity Episcopal Church in Newtown, Connecticut. The painting on the cover of this book was created following this session of Reach Out Camp in June 2014.

For Reflection

1. Where is your story in this story?
2. Where do you see God?
3. What causes you to pause and rethink your previous assumptions?
4. What cries out to you?
5. What calls to you?

Go Deeper

1. Have you ever needed to "crawl under a table" and rip whatever was in your hands into pieces? What caused such an emotion? What helped you come out?
2. When (if ever) have you had a conversation with someone who had been incarcerated?
3. Is there a prison near your home or community? How might you reach out to children and families who have loved ones behind bars?

Rest from Anger

Stephen C. Holton

Our orgy of violence continues and the sadness is unbearable. The Episcopal Church's conference "Reclaiming the Gospel of Peace" was a way forward following the events in Newtown, Connecticut, in December 2012. For this, I wrote a liturgy, "Anointed for Peace" (found on page 176). It is a witness that the gospel works; that we need and can do it ourselves.

Sadly the world gets worse. Now the Middle East explodes. First there were the deaths of the Jewish boys in the Hebron Hills. Then there was the burning death of the Palestinian youngster, the football players on the Gaza Beach, the horrendous deaths in Gaza, the bombing of southern Israel. Now ISIS massacres so many in Syria. Ferguson, Missouri, explodes with the death of Trayvon Martin in August 2014. What do we do? Where do we go? How do we change?

We go to our liturgy. We start with confession. We confess our own violence and face our own pain before addressing the violence around us. We turn to God, who alone can equip us for this ministry. And God does—in easily accessible ways, through our liturgy, in our community—as in generations past.

"Anointed for Peace" is a liturgy I have used in a Harlem community of churches, in a Westchester youth group, for a Memorial Day service, and in "Reclaiming the Gospel of Peace." It begins with the homily "Rest from Anger." Such a worship service

can bring to the surface buried anger, sadness, or pain that participants may think is long gone. But something about familiar words
and a trusted community brings healing. It has always been thus,
since the days of Christ and his disciples. Once healed, we can go
forward—in God's continuing work, of healing our world.

Rest from Anger

It has been a long Holy Week, already, from Newtown until now. It
has been a long period of despair and violence and anger. It began
a long time ago. Perhaps it began back in 33 CE on Golgotha outside
the city wall—always during Holy Week and never Easter.

Perhaps it began a long time before that, just outside of Eden,
where Adam and Eve had been thrust because they had refused to
accept God's sovereignty in the Garden. Because they thought they
could do better themselves—if they just knew enough, and could
plan enough.

If we just knew enough, and could plan enough—does that
sound familiar? Aren't we in an orgy of wondering what we could
have done—as we look at the horrendous acts of violence that
continue on, and on, and on—and then making a plan, and then
doing it, and it's just not enough?

What do we do now? Well, what did we do then? What did
God do then? It is always useful to go back to the Bible, our religious family history, to see what our relatives did when confronted
with similar circumstances.

It all begins with Cain killing his brother Abel in a fit of jealousy (Genesis 4:1-16). And God catches him at it, and drives him
away. In the story, do you notice that the word "brother" is used
six times in eight verses? The Bible really, really pounds it in. This
is not just some guy. This is not to be expected. This is his brother,
his relationship, and his blood. It is not all right. It is not to be
understood, for any reason. It should not have been done!

He is: your brother, your brother, your brother, your brother,
your brother, and your brother.

OK what now? How do we proceed? The ground has cursed
him. God should kill him.

God doesn't. What gives?

God rests from anger. That's right, God rests from anger.

Do you notice that Abel is called Cain's brother *six* times, as
God rams home Cain's extreme guilt? Well, wherever there's a six
in the Bible, there's always a seventh. So what's the seventh?

Well, the seventh thing that happens is: God rests. Isn't that interesting? Isn't that biblical? God rests from anger.

The next thing that happens—after God has established Cain's absolute guilt—is that God does not follow through with the prescribed penalty of death that all creation and the ground itself calls out for.

God rests from anger. He keeps his own Sabbath; and in this way, reclaims the holiness and peace with which he formed the world—instead of letting the predatory actions of human beings set the tone for the future.

Then God does something life-giving, even in that situation. God drives Cain out, but then marks him so that no one will touch him. Then life continues, for everyone.

When we rest from anger, and reclaim holiness and peace, we can do something life giving, and life can begin again, as it did in the very beginning. It cannot "go on." Something too terrible has happened for that. But it can begin again. The world will still be populated, because God rested from anger, and life, not death, was reasserted.

In Jewish mysticism, the day after the end of the week—the Sabbath day—is also the day before the beginning of the next week. It is the day before Creation. It is the day when the Holy One rests over the waters, before the earth comes forth.

When you rest on the Sabbath, you take time out for Eternity. You reenter the primordial soup of Creation. You are born again, each week, ready to start another. It will not overwhelm you with all of its demands. You will overwhelm it with all of your new life.

So God takes a Sabbath rest from anger. And sure enough, new life begins for everybody—for Cain, for Adam and for Eve, and eventually for Seth and for all of Creation. If God had not taken that rest, life would not have begun again. Holiness would not have had a chance to reassert itself. It would have ended just there, and death would have had the last word.

But God did take a rest, and the world brought forth new life. So I invite you, like God, to take a rest! I invite you to sit back, and open your hand, right now, and let go whatever weapon you have been holding close to your heart ever since you were first hurt, or a loved one was first hurt—or ever since you first hurt someone else.

Let go of the weapon.

Now, of course, your hands are open. With open hands, you can receive healing ointment. Then you can truly pass the Peace. You can receive the Eucharist. You can say hello to new friends and old; and you can spread the Gospel of Peace.

This service is all about opening our hands, and putting down the burden of violence, and taking up the Gospel of Peace.

So first, as soon as I finish, you will move around and go to someone you don't know well. One of you will open your hands, as Jesus opened his hands on the cross to receive the nails. And the other will put their downturned hands into your upturned hands. And they will confess all the violence they have done—in thought, word, or deed; in things done and left undone. And they will let the violence drop out. And you will receive them, with a prayer.

Then you will reverse, and the other will confess, and the other will receive.

Then we will do something harder. Each of us will drop the well-deserved anger about the violence done to us—my brother, my brother, my brother—into the other hands, and with God's help, we will forgive.

How do we forgive the unforgiveable? How do we forgive when someone has done something deathly to us or to those we love?

We look at the Bible again. What did Christ do? We look at those last words from the cross, addressed to all those people who had condemned Jesus to death. Jesus looked out and knew that he had to forgive them, but could not. He did not say: "I forgive them, Lord." He said, "Forgive them, Lord, for they know not what they do." He did not forgive them. He asked God to forgive them.

He was not there yet. He knew he had to start the conversation of forgiveness, but he could not start it himself. The people had not even repented! So often, those who have harmed us or those we love have not repented. They do not care. And yet, we know that we have to move on ourselves. In order to allow God's plan for our world to continue, we have to forgive them. But we cannot. We cannot. We cannot. It is just too painful.

But God can. God can release us from the eternal grudge match that the lack of forgiveness condemns us to. So we ask him to do so.

Say Psalm 51, David's penitential psalm. It may feel like the Ash Wednesday liturgy; it is, because it is all about self-examination so we can rejoin the community of the Church. We don't rejoin the faith community so we can stay safe from the world. We rejoin so we can become God's agents in the world, for the unfolding of God's continued plan. For then we will line up and come forward and have our hands anointed for Peace.

Our hands will be anointed with holy oil, as those women at the tomb anointed the body of Jesus, their dear Savior, who was dead by violence. And the oil, the fragrant oil of myrrh that they put on his dear body, would have rubbed off on their hands. And they would have smelled it all the way home. And how can you use those hands—smelling of your sweet and gentle Savior—for violence? They can only be used to shake the hand of a friend, and then to receive Jesus's holy body again in the bread, and feel his new life in ours.

Then life begins again. Then we pass his Peace to a stranger—and so become vessels of Christ's Peace in the world. In that moment of that firm handshake of Peace, we become not strangers anymore, but the neighbors we were meant to be.

Once we have loved God and been loved by God—in prayer and in Sabbath and in Eucharist—that love propels us out into love for our neighbor, whom God also created, and God also loves. Neighborliness is the mission of the Church! It is not just for the neighbors we know, but the neighbors we don't know. It is not just the neighbors in church, but also the neighbors on the street. It is that wonderful Anglican and Episcopal charism that feels a sense of care for everyone in the parish boundaries, for the entire community, and sends us out to love and serve them.

We are called to respect the dignity of every human being, not just those we know or agree with, but *every* human being. By loving them in this way—for respect is a part of love—we build up their dignity, a dignity that no one else may have touched before.

One can only wonder what would have happened in the heart of Adam Lanza in Newtown, and in the lonely heart of his mother, if someone had taken this neighborliness seriously, this very Christian calling seriously, and loved those neighbors as himself or herself.

That was the plan from the beginning. That is the idea starting way back in Eden: to love, and not to know and not even to plan. We reclaim the plan when we take that rest from anger to begin with, and remember that we are about life, not death; and God is about life, not death. And life always begins again, as it did after the cross.

Clench your fist for a moment, in all the very real anger that the evildoers deserve, with the curse that cries out from the very ground. Let go, and open your hand; let the anger fall to the ground. It is then that we can approach Jesus empty-handed, and receive the oil on the spot where he was wounded, and be healed. It is not the last day. It is the first.

As usual, Holy Week gives way to Easter. And those disciples who abandoned Jesus and his Way of the Cross became his apostles in the world. They are united in his Peace once again; and can go in Peace, to love and serve the Lord.

The Reverend Stephen C. Holton is the assistant for Christian formation at St. Barnabas Episcopal Church in Irvington, New York. With a Mission Enterprise Zone grant from the Episcopal Church, he developed Warriors of the Dream, a youth program in Harlem that gathers youth of many faiths with artists, community leaders, and elders to nurture gifts, teach dialogue skills, develop leaders, and build the neighborhood. His liturgy "Anointed for Peace," of which this essay was the meditation, can be found on page 176 in Part Four, Pray: The Work.

For Reflection

1. Where is your story in this story?
2. Where do you see God?
3. What causes you to pause and rethink your previous assumptions?
4. What cries out to you?
5. What calls to you?

Go Deeper

1. Does "liturgy" heal you? If so, how? If not, why not?
2. What does the "mark of Cain" (Genesis 4:15) mean to you?
3. How do we "mark" one another?
4. What weapons do you hold in your heart? How can you let them go?
5. How do we forgive the unforgiveable?
6. What neighbor needs your open hands?

PART III

RECLAIM:
THE RESPONSE

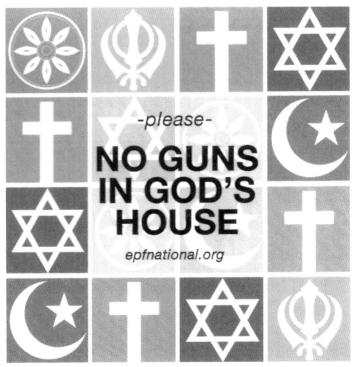

The Prophetic Response
to Violence

Justin Welby

[As we gather here in Oklahoma City] we all have in our minds the sadness and horror that was felt both in the shooting in a post office in 1986 and the attack on the Alfred P. Murrah Building in 1995 in which 168 people were killed and many more injured. And as I come to speak to you this morning, I have the kind of sense that I had in the days when I was a parish priest when one was always conscious that to be invited into someone else's home to talk about things of great importance to them was a privilege and responsibility of an exceptional sort. To be invited to speak to you gives me the same sense of needing to tread gently, with love and deep respect for you and for the thoughtfulness of the churches across this wonderful country.

One brief moment on gun laws and the Second Amendment, and this is one area I want to be clear there are no subliminal messages. In England it is almost impossible to own a firearm and if you're a farmer or somebody who lives out in the country you can get a shotgun permit. But certainly owning a revolver, semiautomatic weapon, or automatic weapon is unheard of. My daughter was a police officer for three years, in a difficult part of London, and during those three years, like all her colleagues, she never once carried a firearm. And that is normal in the police in England. We have firearms officers, but there are very few of them.

We have a totally different culture in the United Kingdom, which springs out of our history and our heritage. We don't have the Second Amendment. It would be extremely discourteous for me to start telling you what I thought the right thing was. In England, that's our position, so you need to understand that any lack of understanding I have of you comes because it's just a totally different approach.

But whether we're talking about the United States or elsewhere, we're talking about a world in which civilian populations now feel the impact of violence more and more widely. The old understanding that in war and civil war you try not to harm civilians has gone by the board. We lost that in the Second World War, if we hadn't lost it in the First. And we also live in a world where in many parts of the world people express themselves, when they run out of other ways to express themselves, with extreme violence.

The catastrophe at Sandy Hook moved not just the United States, but the entire world. We were transfixed with horror.

As Christians we remain committed to concepts of peace and nonviolence wherever possible, and whatever our attitude to firearms. But amongst the churches the definition of "wherever possible we don't use violence" varies very extensively, from total pacifism among certain groups, particularly certain groups of Anabaptists such as the Mennonites, through to a commitment to an Augustinian or Thomist approach to just war. Whatever view we take, I am assuming that no one here feels that early resort to violence is a good thing. The resort to violence is always the denial of the possibility of redemption. And since in our hearts we believe in redemption as Christians, an early resort to violence denies the very heart of our faith.

There are exceptions. . . . One of the managers of the big soccer teams in Liverpool, where I used to live and work, Bill Shankly, was famous for saying: "I always teach my lads to get their retaliation in first." But that is fine on the soccer pitch; it doesn't really work elsewhere. And if we're going to say that early resort to violence is wrong, we always end up with someone saying to us, "But what would you do if . . . ?" In other words, in what way can the Church across the world stand for nonviolence and challenge the resort to violence which seems to be the nature of disputes in everything from neighborhoods to countries? And the Church has typically—and I'm talking about the Church in its broadest sense—tended to wring its hands and to say that the world is a bad place, and then we either stand aside and refuse to participate in structures of violence, or if we do get involved we seek to do so in a way that recognizes the badness of the world and deals with it accordingly. In other words we tend either to take a pietistic approach and pretend it's not there, or we take a compromising approach and get drawn into the very structures that we condemn.

I want to propose a slightly different approach, grounded both in experience and theology, of the prophetic response to violence, which accepts the world as it is and seeks to bring redemption and salvation.

Let me begin with a story. On November 14, 1940, the German Air Force bombed Coventry, a city at the time around two hundred thousand people in the very middle of England. For historic reasons Coventry and the towns around it had always been part of what we might call the industrial complex in the United Kingdom. Significant numbers of factories making new engines, tanks, and other munitions were based in and around the city. At its heart was the thirteenth-century Cathedral of St. Michael, which in the seven hundred years in which it had stood had been at various times a parish church and was then a well-known and very beautiful cathedral. The older parts of Coventry were generally medieval and it was an exceptionally beautiful city.

The bombing lasted eight hours, and together with subsequent raids in 1941, led to the damage or destruction of approaching 80 percent of the houses in the city. Towns and churches around were also hit very heavily. This was the period from mid-1940 to mid-1941, from the British withdrawal at Dunkirk until the entry of the Soviet Union; Europe was hostile or unfriendly neutral from North Cape at the top of Norway to the southern tip of Spain, and it was the lowest and darkest point of the war. On this occasion, not only the city, but also the cathedral was heavily hit. It burned to the ground.

The following morning, the provost, Richard Howard, while walking in the ruins picked up a piece of burnt wood and wrote behind the High Altar the words, "Father forgive." Someone said to him, "You mean Father forgive them?" to which he replied, in the words of Romans 3:23. "No, for all have sinned and fall short of the glory of God." Violence is not something that is only the sin of the other.

On December 25, 1940, Christmas Day, the worst Christmas of the war, Dick Howard was invited to preach the sermon at the main Christmas Day service on the BBC. He did so, and in it he called for postwar reconciliation. It was not a popular call. I met people in Coventry when I was there from 2002 to 2007 who still remember that moment with bitterness and would never again step into the cathedral. The ruins were fresh when he spoke at Christmastime, the bodies scarcely buried in mass graves, the sense of shock of the effect of mass-bombing on a city was still new, although tragically that effect was to wear off over the next five years.

In 1945 soon after the end of the war, Howard sent a group of people from Coventry to Kiel in Germany; and subsequently his successor Bill Williams made contact with Dresden . . . and the link between Coventry and Dresden is today as strong as it was then. When the Frauenkirche, the great church of Dresden, was rebuilt after the fall of the Berlin Wall, the top part was a cross from Coventry.

In 1940, those crosses began to be gathered up from the medieval nails that had fallen from the burning beams. They were made into crosses, of different size depending on the nails. In the years following the war Dick Howard and then Bill Williams set up what were called Communities of the Cross of Nails[38] (CCN) of which there are now nearly two hundred across the world, including nearly twenty in the United States. These communities, based around home groups of one kind or another, were committed to peace and reconciliation and to working out what that meant both in their local community and internationally. It was a major step toward postwar reconciliation, recognized by the German government, by the president of Germany a few years ago; and it means, as a former bishop of Coventry once said to me, "In England I am an unknown provincial bishop, but in Germany I am more important than the archbishop of Canterbury."

The German CCN remains vigorous and growing, tackling many different aspects of reconciliation in all its different forms. The CCN globally is found in such places as Burundi, in Rwanda, in the Middle East, and in the Far East. Most of these are Christian, founded on Christ, although there are some centers of reconciliation which have as their focus a statue of reconciliation by Josefina de Vasconcellos in place of a cross, for example at Hiroshima.

I have told this story at some length because I had the privilege of heading up the CCN work when I was a canon at Coventry Cathedral between 2002 and 2007, and to this day my pectoral cross is one of those original crosses of nails. It is profoundly precious to me as a symbol of the prophetic challenge of the Church to reclaim the Gospel of Peace in the face of the unspeakable violence of war.

---

38   www.crossofnails.org.

In that case the war was global; the violence was legal. How much more can we and should we do today!

Violence in war is something I have spent much of the past ten years confronting. During my time at Coventry full-time and professionally, and since part-time but still developing in understanding of the processes of conflict, from complete ignorance to significant ignorance—and I can tell you that is a progress—I have been involved in mediation and reconciliation work now for over a decade. During that time I have stood by mass graves, most recently in January in the South Sudan with Caroline, where the bodies of murdered and raped clergy and lay leaders from the Cathedral at Bor lay at the feet of Caroline and myself. I have left countries hurriedly when someone saw violence as the best way of dealing with the threat of reconciliation, a deep threat to those who train in the machinery of death; and I have variously rejoiced and most often despaired at the vast number of failures and the very occasional success in challenging cultures of violence.

But certain things are absolutely clear for a church that wishes to challenge violence, to reclaim the Gospel of Peace. They are as true for individuals as societies or churches, as true in war as in neighbourhoods or in families.

First, we have to have a worked through and thoughtful theological anthropology, an understanding of the nature of the human being, if we are to challenge violence effectively.

I recently saw the film *Noah*, which was interesting and thought-provoking. The film actually has some very powerful themes, but one of them is the wickedness of humanity, which is so clearly set out in the narrative in Genesis and is brought out with great power in the film. Humanity is presented as so bad as to be beyond redemption with the exception of Noah and his family. The story ends, of course, with a statement that never again will that decision by God to end humanity be made.

Both of these comments are profoundly theological. They say something about the nature of God and a great deal about the nature of human beings. They recognise that without the intervention of God, human beings are lost. Christianity is not pessimistic, but it is very real about the proclivity of human beings to extreme violence, and the better we get at violence, the more we use it. That is one of the most horrifying lessons of the twentieth century.

In the nineteenth century, the American Civil War was up to that point the bloodiest in terms of proportions of troops killed and wounded that had been seen in history. The unspeakable casualties of that terrible period, and the profound impact of that war on the

United States in the decades and even century and a half that followed, was not because Americans are more violent than anyone else, it is that at the time their industry was more capable than anyone else of producing the means to express the same violence as everyone else was seeking to express in war. They produced better means of killing.

A very few years before the Civil War, the battles of Magenta and Solferino in the Austro-French war around the wars of Italian unification also set such an appalling example of casualties, principally from the development of rapid-firing weapons, that it triggered the formation of the Red Cross. The better we are technically, the better we are at killing. Violence is intrinsic to being human, and I have to say in particular to being human and male, or human and powerful, over against minorities of all kinds.

Moreover it is addictive; violence is addictive, and we become hardened to it. In the seventeenth century during the Fronde, the religious wars in France between 1648 and 1653, a contemporary writer, a senior officer, said that in the first of the three Fronde they had fought like humans, in the second like animals and in the third like demons. To take another example, the bombing of Coventry in 1940 was seen to be an atrocity, but the British bombed Dresden in 1945 without hesitation. Only later, years after the war, were questions asked. I remember only a few years ago, and it will happen next year when I go back, being shown the square in Dresden where the bodies had been piled and where the fire was so great that they spontaneously combusted. War and violence brutalise people. The more often a person is involved in violence, the less atrocious the violence becomes.

The damage violence does to the soul grows deeper and deeper. I remember a meeting last year with my colleague and friend David Porter where we were meeting with some people on opposite sides of a very difficult conflict; and the opening question from David was: "What is this doing to your soul?" It wasn't the question they were expecting; they thought it would be something about practical solutions. What is it doing to your soul? Violence shatters, corrupts, corrodes the soul . . . and violence is profoundly corrosive of all other human restraint. If you are accustomed to killing, then other atrocities such as torture, rape and deliberate mutilation of civilians or prisoners become more tolerable. In particular, as we know, sexual violence accompanies physical violence in almost every conflict on earth and always has done. But today it is used more and more widely as a weapon of war.

The recognition of this bias, of this tendency to sin, seen from the story of Cain and Abel with such vivid reality, is essential if we are going to be churches that challenge violence. You cannot challenge something in which you do not entirely believe, and you cannot treat a disease that you have not properly diagnosed, especially if it is in ourselves. If we recognise that tendencies to violence and the use of more and more violence are part of human life and human nature in its unredeemed state—in this at least Hobbes was right when he talked of the state of civilization being that the life of man is "nasty, brutish, short"—if we believe human nature in its unredeemed state is violent, then the treatment is going to be different to that which we would prescribe if we believe that violence is merely an aberrant tendency in a small minority, or if we believe as good Marxists that it is the means by which a class elite occupy the vast mass of those they rule in order to distract them from inequities and injustices in society. The former leads to repentance, when we see it as our disease; the latter, when it is an aberrant tendency, leads to blame. And that will make no progress.

Secondly, if that is the case, it alters our understanding of the intervention of God in human affairs. It shapes our theology, and theology shapes our mission. The story of Noah speaks of a God who destroys utterly apart from those who have heard his call. God judges but he also saves. In the account of Sodom and Gomorrah, the presence of a few good people may save a greater community. Abraham says to God: "Far be it from you to do such a thing, to slay the righteous with the wicked, so that the righteous fare as the wicked! Far be that from you! Shall not the Judge of all the earth do what is just?"

And in John 3:16, we see the same recognition of human evil (the verse has a presupposition of a universal need for salvation because something has gone universally wrong), but that need is met by God so loving the world that God gives Jesus, the Son of God, so that all who believe in him should not perish but have eternal life. This new ark created by Jesus Christ is picked up in 1 Peter 3 and in Christian iconography as a symbol of the Church, and is a basic understanding of ecclesiology. We are the ark.

So we have a humanity which is committed to doing wrong, and a God who is committed to acting in response to wrongdoing, but following the promise in Genesis, acts through the giving of God's own self to make an opportunity for rescue. And the outcome of this understanding, of both human nature and the action of God, is one of extreme demand for Christians.

Reconciliation and an end to violence, or the transformation of violent conflict into nonviolent conflict (I will come back to that in a moment) is something that can only be achieved by sacrifice and by a prophetic stand. There are no shortcuts and there are no cheap options. We are talking at this point about change in the heart of the human being, and neither technology nor law will alter that.

I spoke a moment ago about reconciliation as the transformation of violent into nonviolent conflict. I take it for granted that diversity, and thus competition, are a natural part of creation. This is in one part natural theology and in another it draws on the recognition found in Scripture from the story of Lot and Abraham to the letters to the Church in Corinth. The work of the Spirit of God in reconciliation is to enable a heart of love to overcome the potential hardness of confrontation, and through generosity, for conflict to be met by grace and gratuity. This means that the zero-sum game of equivalence and exchange, to which Paul Ricoeur refers, becomes transformed through the action of God in to a world of abundance and grace. Diversity then becomes additional not competitive. If I give you something in forgiveness, we both become richer, rather than me poorer and you richer.

Sam Wells, a good friend, rector of St Martin-in-the-Fields, and formerly the dean of Duke University Chapel, in a beautiful lecture at Coventry on reconciliation at the end of February 2013, said this: "Reconciliation isn't about replacing conflict with peace. It's about the transfiguration of conflict into glory." It's about the transfiguration of conflict into glory. Does that not make your heart rise? Does that not sound like what we want in society and in our world?

To speak of a reconciled world is to speak of one in which there is peace (shalom) with God and thus with each other, not unanimity of view. Not a centralised saying "we're all going to do the same thing." Not some kind of Big Brother–esque world. Within the Church, reconciliation enables diversity to result in the flowering of talent and gifting, of a collegial leadership and of the capacity to face every problem with the multiplicity of graciously given talent that lies within the Church.

But reconciliation with God is achieved through the cross, not through conferences and meetings and declarations. The Christian disciple is to take up their cross, and for many even today this is no mere metaphor. Bearing the cross means public ownership of Christ, public association and love with and for all those others who own Christ as Saviour, and public commitment to follow Christ wherever we are taken. There are no choices in a world of bearing one's cross but the choices of sacrifice and the joy that comes in foot-washing, and in yet more cross-bearing.

As well as the language of conflict reconciled, the New Testament uses the language of slavery set free. Redemption, the buying and manumission of the slave, requires risk with those who are being freed, sacrifice of resource by those freeing and suffering to find such a resource. In the Church the suffering may be that of not getting our own way, not having our own will, losing power. That's a tough call in a 1,400-year-old church. We get quite used to the sense of having our own way.

In the world, Christian suffering for redemption will come as a result of other people misunderstanding what we do. Let us have no illusions: real reconciliation is never popular. One of the key reasons for that is our liking for the position of having someone to hate. We like our opposition; it's jolly difficult when you haven't got an enemy. There's a wonderful story by Saki, an English writer killed in battle. He writes one short story of great amusement and insight about a weekend house party where the host invariably invites one person who everyone else will hate because it will make sure the party goes with a swing.

We like having those whom we hate, we like the comforts of defining and distinguishing "us" from "them" in order to bolster our own position. Miroslav Volf, one of my favourite theologians, speaks of Christ as having died for the victim and the perpetrator. It is the last bit that something deep within us rejects. Siding with victims is fine, it's heroic, you get good marks, the press say you're a nice person. But reconcilers must get alongside the perpetrators. The Gospel of Peace is reclaimed by loving those who love violence and hatred.

It is not popular to speak of forgiveness during a war as one city lies burning, like Dick Howard. But the deep tragedy of World War II, and of the cumulative ten years of war between the United Kingdom and Germany in the first half of the last century, in which those two countries alone killed several million of each other's citizens, that tragedy began to be redeemed on the day that Dick Howard wrote "Father forgive" on the ruined wall of Coventry Cathedral. We prefer to win wars, we prefer to win wars against violence, and to defeat our dehumanised enemy than to find the reconciliation that is the true victory of the Gospel of Peace.

So in conclusion, what does a church committed to reclaiming the Gospel of Peace look like? What does it look like in the United States where there are people who are faithful Christians on all sides of the debate about guns? What does it mean to be a faithful Christian? What it does not mean is to shout louder from your corner in the conviction that you are right and everyone else is stupid.

Rather, a church committed to the reclaiming of the Gospel of Peace looks like those who join their enemies on their knees. We celebrate the fact that as the Anglican Communion functioning as a community of peace across the world, which it does in so many places so wonderfully with such sacrifice, that it manages disagreement well in many places, that it maintains unity across diametrically opposed views on a matter—that that Anglican Communion to which we belong could be the greatest gift to counter violence of all descriptions in our world. That is the goal and the hope of reclaiming the Gospel of Peace, that we are those who enable that transfiguration into glory in the grace of God.

Practically, a church that reclaims the Gospel of Peace is a church that is present with those who are poorest and suffer most, and gives them priority, whether close to home or far away. Being with the poor and suffering changes us. If you want to see this set out in a book of great beauty and very demanding discussion, have a look at Sam Wells and Marcia A. Owen, *Living Without Enemies* (IVP, 2011).

Being with the poor and suffering changes us. Being with them changes us. Not doing things for them, doing things to them, working for them—that may matter—but being with them changes us.

We find it easier as individuals, especially those in the relatively prosperous and secure global north, to work for people, and occasionally work with people. We bring answers; we solve problems. Once we move beyond the individual to the institutional level the language of outcomes dominates, and the drive for results prevails. But Jesus came to spend much of his life being with us, and only a little working for us. To be with is to take up the cross and walk with the poor, and prefer their cry to that of the powerful.

In the South Sudan and DRC a few weeks ago Caroline and I found ourselves faced with the immense suffering of the poorest people in the world. In one of the IDP camps, surrounded by death and dying, where every hope seemed vain, the bishop said, "Say something to encourage them." I blurted out, "Jesus Christ is the same yesterday, today and forever" and found I had accidentally—and I stress accidentally—said the right thing, while actually mentally searching for the right solution. Being with them, and all of us with Christ, was what we all needed most at that moment.

On Sunday I was with Cardinal Nichols, the leader of the Catholic Church in the UK, in a home for asylum seekers. And in May I will have the privilege of being with a church school as it launches the Church of England's national policy against homophobic bullying in our schools.

On each of those days I know I will be tempted to ask myself what I have done, and I know that that is the wrong question. I need to answer the question: "With whom have I been, and with whom has the church been?" Of course action and programs are essential, utterly essential, but reclaiming the Gospel of Peace means being with others who are poor as I am poor and the church is poor and together being on the ground where the Gospel of Peace is reclaimed.

The gospel is good news for the poor. Far from those places of which I have spoken, here in the United States you look at questions of gun law and violence. Perhaps part of the answer is not only advocacy, and that must happen, but being on knees together with the poorest and the most vulnerable in your local communities, of being with them so that they are also with the church when it is with the powerful, because we have that great privilege. Already this is happening all over the United States with the Episcopal Church. May God bless that being with, as well as all the working for.

So we seek a church that bears the cross, that is so caught up in Jesus Christ and its relationship with Jesus Christ that it is drawn inexorably in partnership with the poor and pilgrimage alongside them, sharing the surprises and risks of the journey under the leadership of Jesus Christ. We seek a church pursuing the will of God, a church that demonstrates its unity, love, and action "that the world may believe that you have sent me" (John 17: 21).

We do not see such churches today on a global scale, although they may be found in many places at a local level. To turn this into a national effort in such a great and huge nation as this, let alone a global phenomenon, is humanly impossible. We find it easier to be caught up in our own disputes and our own rights.

But as we approach Easter, it is in accompanying Jesus on the long walk through Holy Week to the cross that we will find ourselves bound together afresh and love released. The love will be such that we cannot imagine unless we turn to Christ in repentance, seeking to be those who challenge and overcome the violence that he himself bore for us on the cross. It will be a love that comes to reclaim in ourselves and in our communities the Gospel of Peace.

The Most Reverend Justin Welby is the 105th archbishop of Canterbury. For twenty years, his ministry has blended deep devotion to his parish communities with church work around the world, especially in areas of conflict. He attended the "Reclaiming the Gospel of Peace" conference and offered this address on April 10, 2014.

For Reflection

1. Where is your story in this story?
2. Where do you see God?
3. What causes you to pause and rethink your previous assumptions?
4. What cries out to you?
5. What calls to you?

Go Deeper

1. What do you think it means that "since in our hearts we believe in redemption as Christians, an early resort to violence denies the very heart of our faith"?
2. In what way can the Church across the world stand for non-violence and challenge the resort to violence which seems to be the nature of disputes in everything from neighborhoods to countries?
3. What is your understanding of the nature of the human being? Is violence intrinsic to being human?
4. Do you believe war and violence can brutalize people over time? How so?
5. The work of the Spirit of God in reconciliation is to enable a heart of love to overcome the potential hardness of confrontation, and through generosity, for conflict to be met by grace and gratuity. How does one accomplish this?
6. What does a church committed to reclaiming the Gospel of Peace look like? What does it look like in the United States where there are people who are faithful Christians on all sides of the debate about guns? What does it mean to be a faithful Christian?

There Are Ways to Prevent This

Mariann Edgar Budde

> *Do not be overcome by evil; but overcome evil with good.* (Romans 12:21)

A journalist in Arizona called to ask if I had any thoughts on how Richard Martinez, the outspoken father of a young man killed in last Friday's shooting in Isla Vista, California, could craft a persuasive gun control message. In his grief, Martinez has said that he is determined to speak and to act until something changes. But the journalist had her doubts. Angry, grieving families and rising body counts aren't persuading those opposed to measures such as universal background checks, limits on high capacity magazines, stricter gun trafficking laws, a reinstatement of the assault weapons ban, and addressing the inadequacies of our mental healthcare system.

"I've been following the gun legislation debates since Arizona congresswoman Gabriel Giffords was shot three years ago," she told me. Nothing has changed. I told her that many of the religious leaders who took up the cause for sensible gun legislation in the aftermath of the Sandy Hook Elementary School killings, including me, thought that the tide was turning, and that we could finally overcome those who financially benefit from the sale and illegal trafficking of increasingly lethal guns. We were wrong.

While small gains have been made in some places, to date, we haven't been able to move national legislation. And so the shooting continues, every day, somewhere, as if this were normal; as if, in the words of the satirical newspaper *The Onion,* there is "No Way to Prevent This."[39]

And yet, I told her, if you want to understand the kind of work we're engaged in, think back on other changes that we take for granted now that seemed impossible as people fought for them. When you watch an episode of *Mad Men* or a movie from the 1960s, you see people chain-smoking cigarettes everywhere. Do you remember how impossible it felt to change laws that affected our smoking habits?

Or consider, I said, the long struggle for basic civil rights for African-Americans and other citizens of color in this country. While we have a long way to go toward the goal of racial equality, fifty years ago people were beaten, arrested, and even killed for trying to integrate restaurants and buses. Can you imagine living in that America now?

Or remember even as recently as a decade ago, when the idea of marriage equality for gays and lesbians was unimaginable, and the forces opposed to gay marriage—even the most basic of civil unions—prevailed in the cultural debate. That tide has turned in ways that even the most ardent, hopeful marriage equality advocate of ten years ago would have found hard to imagine.

Did we all suddenly wake up one morning and change our minds? Did our politicians decide on their own to vote differently? Of course not. Social change is always slow and incremental at first. For years, often decades, people struggle with seemingly nothing to show for their efforts. Looking back, we recognize hinge moments, when things seemed to shift quickly and dramatically. But never did those shifts occur separate from the hard and strategic work of organizing and of shifting the moral center of debate.

That's what happening now. Even as the killings continue, we are organizing across the country, and each day the coalition grows stronger. Richard Martinez, in his grief, is now part of the growing movement that will one day prevail in seeing our gun laws change. I'm proud to be part of that movement and to stand alongside so many of you.

In years to come, we will look back on this time and wonder how we could have possibly accepted this level of gun violence.

---

39   "'No Way To Prevent This,' Says Only Nation Where This Regularly Happens," *The Onion* 50 (May 27, 2014): 21.

Just as we think in horror now on parts of our past, our children's children will shake their heads in disbelief that we took as long as we did to end this public health epidemic during which, on average, two mass shootings occur every month and over thirty thousand Americans die each year by guns. But until that time, the work continues. There are ways to prevent this, and we know it.

The Right Reverend Mariann Edgar Budde was consecrated the ninth bishop of the Diocese of Washington in November 2011. This article appeared on her blog on Thursday, May 29, 2014, following the May 23rd shooting rampage in Isla Vista, California, near the campus of the University of California in Santa Barbara that killed six people and injured thirteen others.

For Reflection
1. Where is your story in this story?
2. Where do you see God?
3. What causes you to pause and rethink your previous assumptions?
4. What cries out to you?
5. What calls to you?

Go Deeper
1. Looking back, what hinge moments have you experienced in your life, when things seemed to shift quickly and dramatically?
2. What do you believe constitutes the hard and strategic work of organizing and of shifting the moral center of debate on gun violence in the United States?

17

Gun Laws Save Lives

Daniel W. Webster

Federal law identifies a number of conditions that prohibit an individual from purchasing or possessing firearms. These include having been convicted of a felony crime or a misdemeanor domestic assault, being subject to a restraining order for domestic violence (with important exceptions), having been adjudicated to be dangerous as a result of mental illness, and abusing illegal drugs. The minimum legal age requirement for receiving a handgun under federal law is twenty-one years if the seller is a federally licensed gun dealer and eighteen years if the transaction is with an unlicensed private seller. There is evidence linking each of these prohibiting conditions to increased risk for committing violence and for several additional prohibiting conditions set in some states' laws.[40]

There is a glaring weakness in federal laws and in most states' laws that are designed to prevent prohibited persons from accessing firearms. Prospective firearm purchasers must pass a background check verifying that they meet all eligibility requirements if the seller is a federally licensed firearm dealer. But prohibited persons

---

40 Consortium for Risk-Based Firearm Policy, *Guns, Public Health, and Mental Illness: An Evidence-Based Approach for State Policy,* December 2, 2013. http://www.jhsph. edu/research/centers-and-institutes/johns-hopkins-center-for-gun-policy-and-research/ publications/GPHMI-State.pdf.

or anyone who does not want records linking themselves to a gun can acquire firearms from unlicensed private sellers who have no legal obligation to verify that the prospective purchaser can legally possess a firearm.

An effective background check system obviously depends on data on the prohibiting conditions getting into the databases that are checked for gun purchaser screening. Much attention has been given to the need to improve the FBI's National Instant Check System (NICS) by getting all records for disqualifying conditions into the system, especially mental health and domestic violence disqualifications. Yet there has been little consideration of the accuracy of the information submitted for firearm purchase applications. Federal law places licensed firearms dealers and their employees with the responsibility of verifying the authenticity of their customers' government-issued identification cards and the accuracy of the information submitted to law enforcement agencies for background checks. The General Accounting Office conducted a study to test the ability of licensed gun dealers to identify fake drivers' licenses in six states and did not find a single instance in which a dealer questioned authenticity of the fake IDs, causing them to question the soundness of the current system for screening prospective gun purchasers.

Keeping Guns Out of the Wrong Hands

Handgun purchaser licensing laws, also known as Permit-to-Purchase (PTP) laws, have been enacted in eleven states and the District of Columbia. Permits or licenses to purchase firearms are issued after applicants apply with a state or local law enforcement agency and pass a background check. The table below provides details pertinent to the PTP laws currently in effect in eleven states and the District of Columbia. In eight states, individuals must apply in person through a law enforcement agency, and in six states, applicants are fingerprinted. Requiring direct contact with law enforcement likely serves as a deterrent to straw purchasers (individuals who buy a firearm on the behalf of someone else who is disqualified from possession) and, along with fingerprinting, ensures that the identity of the prospective purchaser is verified. In all states with PTP laws, both licensed and unlicensed firearm sellers can only legally sell a firearm to someone if they have a valid PTP or license.

States with handgun purchaser licensing laws tend to have stricter standards for legal gun ownership than do states that don't license handgun purchasers. For example, among the eleven states and the District of Columbia with handgun purchaser licensing laws, nine states and DC set twenty-one as the minimum legal age for handgun purchase. In contrast, only two of the remaining thirty-nine states do so. Three states with handgun purchaser licensing (MA, NJ, NY) also allow law enforcement to use their discretion to deny a license to an applicant if they believe doing so is in the interest of public safety (e.g., history of arrests but no disqualifying conviction).

State	Issuing Agency	Agency Discretion to Deny a Permit	Method of Application	Fingerprints taken	Maximum Wait	Duration of Permit	Safety Training/ Exam
Connecticut	Department of Emergency Services and Public Protection	No	In-person	Yes	Notification within 90 days	5 years	Yes
Hawaii	County Chief of Police	No	In-person	Yes	14 days, process closed after 20 days	10 days	Yes
Illinois	State Police	No	Mail	No	Max. 30 days	5 years	No
Iowa	County Sheriff	No	In-person	No	3 days	1 year	No
Maryland	State Police Department	No	In-person[1]	Yes		10 years	Yes
Massachusetts	Municipal Police Department	Yes	In-person	Yes	40 days	10 days for permit	Yes
Michigan	Local Police or Sheriff Department	No	In-person	No	None	10 days for permit	Yes
Nebraska	County Sheriff Department	No	In-person	No	None	3 years	No
New Jersey	Municipal Police Department	Yes	In-person	Yes	Notification within 30–45 days	90 days	No
New York	Both local and state police vet and issue permits	Yes	In-person	Yes	6 months	Varies by county[2]	No
North Carolina	County Sheriff Department	No	Mail	No	Notification within 30 days	5 years	No
District of Columbia	Metropolitan Police Department	No	In-person	Yes	?	?	No

1   Applicants apply at state government certified vendors who take applicants' fingerprints.

2   Three years in NYC; five years in Nassau, Suffolk, and Westchester Counties; until revoked elsewhere.

Preventing Guns from Being Diverted to Criminals

Studies have demonstrated that states with handgun purchaser licensing laws have lower rates of guns being diverted to criminals shortly after retail sale and lower rates of exporting guns to criminals in other states. A study of guns traced to crime in fifty-three cities that examined intrastate diversion of guns to criminals found that the strongest forms of these laws were associated with 64 percent lower risk of guns being diverted guns to criminals compared to states without such laws.[41] A subsequent study used gun trace data aggregated at the state level and found that PTP laws requiring fingerprinting of applicants were among the most effective state policies to reduce diversions of guns to criminals across state borders. PTP laws that gave law enforcement discretion in issuing permits were associated with 76 percent lower per capita rates of exporting guns to criminals while PTP laws that did not allow discretion but still required fingerprinting of purchasers were associated with 45 percent lower rates of exporting guns to criminals in other states.[42]

There has only been one state PTP licensing law change since relatively good crime gun trace data have been available to systematically examine whether indicators of diversion change with the laws. Missouri lawmakers repealed their state's PTP law effective August 28, 2007. As a result, handgun transactions involving unlicensed sellers no longer required a background check and handgun sales by licensed gun dealers no longer required a presale trip by prospective purchasers to the local sheriff's office for permit application. After Missouri's PTP law was repealed, the share of guns recovered from criminals that moved swiftly from a retail sale to crime involvement doubled and the share of crime guns that had originated from an in-state retail transaction doubled.[43]

---

41 D.W. Webster, J. S. Vernick, and M. T. Bulzacchelli, "Effects of State-Level Firearm Seller Accountability Policies on Firearms Trafficking," *Journal of Urban Health* 86 (2009): 525–37.

42 D. W. Webster, J. S. Vernick, E. E. McGinty, and T. Alcorn, "Preventing the Diversion of Guns to Criminals through Effective Firearm Sales Laws.," in *Reducing Gun Violence in America: Informing Policy with Evidence and Analysis,* ed. Daniel W. Webster and Jon S. Vernick (Baltimore, MD: Johns Hopkins University Press, 2013), 109–22.

43 *Ibid.*

Handgun Purchaser Licensing Linked to Lower Gun-Related Deaths

States with PTP laws tend to have lower firearm-related death rates than states without these laws after controlling for demographic, economic, and other differences across states.[44] A recent study, which examined changes in suicide rates in response to changes in state firearm policies, found that PTP laws reduced suicide rates.[45]

Johns Hopkins researchers recently published a study to estimate the effect of Missouri's repeal of its PTP law on murder rates. We found that firearm-related homicide rates increased abruptly following the law's repeal and was 25 percent higher in the first three years post repeal than was the case during the prior nine years. This sharp increase in firearm homicide rates in Missouri was unusual because none of the states bordering Missouri nor the nation as a whole experienced significant increases in firearm homicide rates during that time period. Substantial increases in firearm homicides were observed in urban and suburban counties throughout the state. Regression analyses controlled for a variety of factors that might account for sharp increases in homicide rates (policing levels, incarceration rates, poverty, unemployment, and other changes in public policies). The law's repeal was associated with a 14 percent increase in Missouri's murder rates through 2012 (about fifty lives per year) and a 25 percent increase in firearm homicides through 2010. There were no changes in homicides committed by means other than firearms.[46]

Public Support for Laws Licensing Handgun Purchasers

Support for background checks for virtually all firearms sales is very wide—90 percent overall and 82 percent among gun owners. A study conducted by Johns Hopkins researchers in January 2013

44   E. W. Fleegler, L. K. Lee, M. C. Monuteaux, D. Hemenway, and R. Mannix, "Firearm Legislation and Firearm-Related Fatalities in the United States," *JAMA Intern Med.* 173 (2013): 732–40.

45   A. R. Andres and K. Hempstead, "Gun Control and Suicide: The Impact of State Firearm Regulations in the United States, 1995–2004," *Health Policy* 101 (2011): 95–103.

46   D. W. Webster, C. K. Crifasi, and J. S. Vernick, "Effects of Missouri's Repeal of Its Handgun Purchaser Licensing Law on Homicides," *Journal of Urban Health* 91 (2014): 293–302.

found that more than three-quarters of adults surveyed supported laws that require prospective firearm purchasers to acquire a license from local law enforcement and nearly six out of ten gun owners supported this policy.[47]

Daniel W. Webster, ScD, MPH, is professor of health policy and management and directs the PhD program in health and public policy at the Johns Hopkins Bloomberg School of Public Health. Dr. Webster is director of the Johns Hopkins Center for Gun Policy and Research, deputy director for research for the Johns Hopkins Center for the Prevention of Youth Violence, and core faculty of the Johns Hopkins Center for Injury Research and Policy. One of the nation's leading experts on firearm policy and the prevention of gun violence, he has studied the effects of a variety of violence prevention interventions, including state firearm and alcohol policies, policing strategies, street outreach and conflict mediation, public education campaigns, and school-based curricula.

For Reflection

1. Where is your story in this story?
2. Where do you see God?
3. What causes you to pause and rethink your previous assumptions?
4. What cries out to you?
5. What calls to you?

Go Deeper

1. What are the gun laws and restrictions in your state?
2. What, if any, statements have your church (or diocese) made about the carrying of weapons into church facilities?
3. How might these statistics help you in your advocacy ministry?

---

47   C. L. Barry, E. E. McGinty, J. S. Vernick, and D. W. Webster, "After Newtown—Public Opinion on Gun Policy and Mental Illness," *New England Journal of Medicine* 368 (2013): 1077–81.

18

B-PEACE for Jorge: A Diocesan-Wide Antiviolence Campaign

Julia MacMahon

I have chosen to devote my professional life to addressing the issue of violence because I am filled with compassion for the families and communities suffering the most from this shameful loss of life. I lost my mother to breast cancer when I was only four years old, so I know what it is like to grow up with a profound sense of loss. I see this pain reflected in the eyes of the younger siblings and friends of the victims of violence whom I have known. I have worked with youth in a variety of settings, ranging from a juvenile detention center to a college-based youth leadership program. I have seen firsthand that young people can be leaders who are part of the solution. I have also seen what it does to a community when this leadership is robbed through an act of violence. And, tragically, over my career I have known personally and been connected indirectly to many young people who have senselessly lost their lives, including Jorge Fuentes, who was killed by a gun on September 10, 2012.

Jorge Fuentes was a truly remarkable young man who I met 6 ½ years ago in the B-SAFE Summer Program run by St. Stephen's Episcopal Church in Boston. Jorge had grown up in the B-SAFE Program and the afterschool programs run by

St. Stephen's and had come up through the ranks so to speak—as a member of the middle school leadership program, teen jobs and enrichment program, and finally as a young adult staff member in the summers. Throughout his time at St. Stephen's, Jorge had transformed from a hardheaded kid to a leader who was looked up to by younger children, admired by his peers, and respected by older teens. He was such a leader that, the summer before he was killed, Jorge worked as a lead counselor at B-SAFE, leading a group of fifteen second graders through a summer of fun and learning, which was a position normally reserved for staff at least two years older than Jorge was at the time.

Because of this, and his charismatic personality, Jorge was well known throughout the Diocese of Massachusetts. Members of suburban partner churches, who would come in to serve lunch to the children or host field trips throughout the years, knew Jorge and looked for him upon arrival. He had joined suburban teens to serve on mission trips to Appalachia and the Gulf Coast and forged friendships with them. Bishop Tom Shaw knew Jorge as the type of young man to speak truth to power. Jorge asked the hard questions like, "Can the Diocese give us ten million dollars to build a teen center?"

Jorge's exemplary leadership made it even more tragic when his life was violently taken eighteen months ago. He was walking his dog and talking to his friend across the street from his home when an unknown teen fired five shots. Our hearts were broken. Over 1,200 people came to Jorge's wake and funeral. For many of his family, friends, and the kids from St. Stephen's youth programs, this was not the first time they had been to such a funeral. But for many of the people who came from those suburban Episcopal churches, this was an awful and new experience. What we witnessed was that there was no difference in grief or the showing of support—all of us were part of the same community of sorrow. As a result of Jorge's involvement in the B-SAFE programs, his death brought about a remarkable transformation in our diocese's understanding of the issue of gun violence—it moved from being an issue impacting "them" to one impacting "us." No longer could people feel only a remote sadness about the violence happening in urban areas, because now they could see how we are all so connected, across geography, across class, and across difference. Even as we grieved this terrible loss, we heard a call to action. In his homily for Jorge, the Reverend Tim Crellin, vicar of St. Stephen's, said:

> We are going to work together to make sure that Jorge's death is not just another statistic in the sad history of

violence in our city, but rather a turning point. This was not an unknown male. This was Jorge Luis Fuentes, our friend, our son, our brother, our coworker. . . . It is horrible that he died, but it is so good that he lived, and we will honor his life by our witness and our work.

I, and hundreds of others from across the diocese heard this call for peace and justice, and the B-PEACE for Jorge Campaign is our response. B-PEACE was launched to give opportunities for all people in the Episcopal Diocese of Massachusetts to take an active role in addressing the root causes of violence. B-PEACE stands for:

Bishop's Action Steps toward Peace:
Programs for youth
Employment for teens and young adults
Academic excellence in public high schools
Communities for families
End to gun violence through meaningful gun reform

Before launching the campaign, we conducted research and interviews to determine the best steps forward. We met with leaders in Baltimore, Washington, DC, Chicago, New Orleans, and the San Francisco Bay area. We held nearly one hundred one-on-one meetings with leaders and experts. We identified national faith-based models and local collaborators, including the Episcopal Peace Fellowship, Massachusetts Coalition to Prevent Gun Violence, and the Episcopal Diocese of Western Massachusetts. After three months of research and conversation, we launched into action and have had many victories in the last eighteen months:

- Over sixty congregations engaged in a book study on *The Rich and the Rest of Us* by Cornel West and Tavis Smiley, discussing how poverty and racism create an environment for violence.
- We held a Diocesan Resource Day with over 350 Episcopalians and others, who attended workshops that helped participants to get involved in our campaign. The Reverend Kathie Adams-Shepherd from Trinity, Newtown, Connecticut, gave the keynote address.
- Members of our Youth and Family Engagement subcommittee have been trained in the STAR model, which stands for Strategies for Trauma Awareness and Resilience, and they will share this model with our

clergy, youth ministers, community partners, and youth groups.

- A grant was received for a part-time youth organizer from the Boston Foundation in September 2013. This person works with young people to develop leadership capacity to organize against gun violence that includes collaborative art, serving as a youth voice at coalition and task force meetings, visiting with youth groups throughout the diocese, and hosting youth-centered leadership events, including a "Lock-In for Peace" held in May 2014.
- Clergy and business leaders were engaged to create fifty-five new jobs for teenagers in the summer of 2013 and are working toward our goal of one hundred new jobs for the summer of 2014. Jobs curb violence.
- We held a Day of Action with the Edison K-8 School with over fifty volunteers to launch a church-school partnership. We have also started a small-scale leadership training program with the 9th grade Student Council at Madison Park Technical Vocational High School, which is Jorge's alma mater.
- Our diocese is a founding member of the Massachusetts Coalition to Prevent Gun Violence and we have a seat on their steering committee. We have organized over one hundred Episcopalians to attend legislative hearings and lobby days on the issue. We took the leadership in organizing interfaith clergy panels for each of the hearings, which included testimony from Bishop Douglas Fisher of the Diocese of Western Massachusetts and several priests from that diocese. We continue to work with this Coalition as we push for an effective bill that will strengthen our gun laws, especially those that we believe will limit the easy access to guns in urban areas.
- Finally, one of the most transformative events that we have joined was the Mother's Day Walk for Peace, a march that has been run by the Louis D. Brown Peace Institute for seventeen years now. Every year they march with families who have lost their loved ones to violence and use this opportunity to bear witness to the violence and create solutions in the city of Boston. Last year, we had the largest showing of any group ever at the walk, with over six hundred and fifty Episcopalians from over sixty-five congregations marching together in the rain, wearing our lavender B-PEACE T-shirts with Jorge's face

on them. After the walk, Bishop Shaw presided over a Eucharist in the park and we were joined by dozens of non-Episcopalians to worship and remember together. The Peace Institute has since used our involvement as a way to encourage other churches and faith groups to join. It was a deeply meaningful moment for all.

We have achieved this success for several reasons: (1) For our diocese, this was personal. We lost one of our own and we felt a strong need to do something about it. When we have faced challenges, Jorge's memory has pushed us to continue. (2) We had the strong prophetic and financial support of our bishops and our Diocesan Council from the very beginning. We saw the crisis of violence that our nation and communities face and this work was made a priority. Our leaders saw this as a chance to put their faith into action and to be the hands and feet of Christ in this world. (3) We took the time to identify the leaders in our state who had already been doing this work and made the effort to collaborate with them, rather than trying to create our own unique responses to violence.

Julia MacMahon is the lead organizer for B-PEACE for Jorge Campaign (www.diomass.org/b-peace). Julia has over ten years of experience, including work in juvenile detention centers, administrative support in public and charter high schools, and serving as a fellow in the prestigious FAO Schwarz Family Foundation Fellowship program. Her passion for youth work began when she served as a corps member and service leader for City Year Washington, DC, directly after high school. In 2009, Julia was selected as a community fellow for Marshall Ganz's widely respected course, "Organizing: People, Power, and Change," at the Harvard University Kennedy School of Government.

For Reflection

1. Where is your story in this story?
2. Where do you see God?
3. What causes you to pause and rethink your previous assumptions?
4. What cries out to you?
5. What calls to you?

Go Deeper

1. Who might you collaborate with in making change?
2. Who has the decision-making power in your community?
3. What are the resources in your community to develop such a grassroots coalition?
4. What research and plan might you begin to dream into a reality?

19

Respecting the Dignity of Those Impacted by Intimate Partner Violence

Robin Hammeal-Urban

Abusive partners and their victims are members of our congregations. They are wardens, vestry members, committee chairs, church school teachers, and choir members. They can be ordained leaders. Other abusive partners and their victims, who are not members of our congregations, live and work in the communities surrounding our churches. As baptized Christians we promise, with God's help, to "proclaim by word and example the Good News of God in Christ . . . seek and serve Christ in all persons, loving [our] neighbors as [ourselves] . . . [and] to strive for justice and peace among all people, and respect the dignity of every human being."[48] How can we do any of this if we are blind as to victims or perpetrators of Intimate Partner Violence (IPV) who not only live in our communities, but worship with us?

As Christians, we are called to engage in God's mission of bringing the brokenness of this world to wholeness, and restoring all to God. Some of the most broken of human relationships are those in which a person perpetrates violence, in any form, against another.

---

48 BCP, 305.

The Dynamics of IPV

Intimate partner violence (IPV) is a pattern of coercive control over an intimate partner characterized by the use of physically, sexually, or psychologically abusive behaviors. Formerly referred to as domestic violence, IPV more accurately describes the phenomenon, as it is violence between intimate partners—not other members of a household or family. Both men and women can be abusive partners, and both can be victims of IPV. IPV occurs in heterosexual relationships and gay and lesbian relationships,[49] with the majority of IPV perpetrated by men against women.[50]

The abusive behaviors used to control another person involve all forms of violence—not only physical violence. An abusive partner may isolate the victim from family and friends by controlling access to the car or phone. The abusive partner may disseminate untruths about those friends and family—"You're better than they are, they will bring you down. I'm the only one who loves and supports you," "They just don't like me and will turn you away from me," or, "If you leave me, your family will side with me." The abusive partner may control access to money, and/or prevent the victim from going to work by keeping her up all night so she cannot perform at work; he may slash all her work clothes in the closet, or fail to care for their children while she works after having promised to do so. Some victims are prevented from applying for a job by being told, "No one will hire you, you're too fat, ugly, stupid . . ." This type of emotional abuse can prevent victims from taking steps to better their lives and become more independent of the abusive partner.

Many victims report that it is much harder to overcome the effects of emotional abuse than those of physical abuse. Bones heal, bruises disappear, and while some physical scarring may remain, that may be easier to overcome than years of being yelled at and told you aren't worthy because you are fat, stupid, or crazy. These may be the only messages a victim hears about herself because she is isolated from friends and family.

---

49 There is some indication that IPV in gay and lesbian relationships is even more underreported than IPV in heterosexual relationships. This may be because there are fewer services available for gay and lesbian victims, and a reticence to recognize that IPV is an issue in these communities.

50 Although both genders can be victims of IPV, female pronouns are used to refer to victims of IPV. This is not to ignore male victims of IPV, but to enhance readability and reflect that the vast majority of victims are women.

In relationships with IPV, not every day involves victimization by physical violence. In fact there are some days when it feels good to be in the relationship. This is because there is a cycle of physical violence. The pattern of coercive control through physical violence is generally cyclical. Usually depicted as a circle with three phases, the cycle starts with a tension building phase in which there is no physical violence, but a sense that it is coming. This is followed by an incident of battering involving physical violence. From both the victim's and abusive partner's perspective, this incident of battering is usually triggered by something the victim did or did not do as the abusive partner would like; it could be dinner wasn't ready on time, it might be talking back to the abusive partner, or even threatening to leave the relationship.

The third and final phase of the cycle of violence is the "honeymoon phase." In this phase the abusive partner shows remorse (which may be genuine), promises it won't happen again, and goes out of the way to treat the abused partner well. Unfortunately, this phase does not last and is followed by the tension-building phase.

Abusive partners and their victims come from all socioeconomic classes, education levels,[51] races and religions, and reflect a wide age span, ranging from teens through old age. Among teens and young adults, it appears that violence occurs in up to 25 percent of dating relationships; the incidence of violence tends to go up in positive correlation with the number of dating partners and dating frequency, and in negative correlation with high grade point averages. Perhaps most alarming is that a significant percentage of victims and abusive partners (25 percent to 30 percent respectively) interpret violence in a relationship as a sign of love! Among elders, IPV may have been present throughout the life of a long relationship, or it can begin later in the relationship when one partner becomes more dependent on the other due to illness or disability—in essence there is a shift in the balance of power; what was a healthy, loving relationship between mutual and equal partners shifts, sometimes suddenly, to a relationship with some degree of dependence. This shift in power results in a loss of the valued partnership, and a burden of dependency, which can lead to resentment and contribute to IPV.

---

51 Interestingly, some studies have shown that women with advanced degrees may be at higher risk of IPV than those will less education.

History and Trends of Partner Violence

Historically, men had the right to use physical violence to chastise their wives. The church endorsed beating one's wife as an acceptable means of correcting her faults in England in the 1200s. Our judicial system in the United States condoned physical abuse as a means of improving the behavior of one's wife. In 1824, in *Bradley v. State of Mississippi*, Calvin Bradley was convicted of assault and battery of his wife because he went beyond what would have been "reasonable chastisement" of his wife. Although Bradley was held accountable, the court's decision affirmed the right of husbands to use a certain degree of physical violence as "reasonable chastisement" of wives.

In two separate cases in 1871, the courts ruled that a man did not have the right to physically abuse his wife. However, these courts, one in Alabama and the other in Massachusetts, did not impose criminal penalties on these husbands. The wife in the Massachusetts case was hit in the face and head to chastise her for being drunk. She fell, hit her head, and died as a result of the fall. The progression of providing women with equal protection under our laws continued to progress, albeit slowly.

On a cultural level, there began to be some recognition that beating one's wife was unacceptable.[52] In 1973 the first battered women's shelter opened in St. Paul, Minnesota. By 1979 there were over 250 shelters, and 700 by 1983. We began to respond to the need for women to have a place to go when they fled their homes to seek safety. The laws to make those homes safe lagged behind the need.

Police response to calls for domestic violence varied greatly. A typical law enforcement response included arriving at the home, separating the partners, and sending the husband out to walk around the block to cool off. The officer might warn the husband, "I don't want to have to come back here again tonight." The law did not require police officers to make an arrest when there was

---

52 As of the time of this writing, the issue of the National Football League's suspension of Ray Rice for having punched his then fiancée in the head while in a public elevator is the lead story on the news. Many fans support Rice and say that this is a private matter between a husband and wife. This begs the question: What if the person Rice punched on the elevator and dragged out unconscious had been a stranger? Such a scenario would have likely prompted an immediate criminal investigation and clarified for all that the behavior of intentionally punching any person in the face is a criminal act.

probable cause that a family violence crime had occurred. That began to change in 1986.

Tracey Thurman lived in Torrington, Connecticut, and had suffered months of physical abuse from her husband. She had numerous court restraining orders that required her husband to stay away from her. Her husband's violence had increased after she told him she would be leaving the marriage. She had called the police many times—their responses were not timely. On June 10, 1983, Tracey was with their 22-month-old son when her husband came to her apartment. She called the police. On this day it took the police twenty-five minutes to arrive. During that time Tracey was stabbed thirteen times, kicked in the head, and had her neck repeatedly stepped on by her husband. Tracy lived; she is permanently disabled from the attack. She sued the police department claiming that she was denied equal protection under the law when they ignored her calls for help because she was married to the perpetrator of the crimes against her. In 1986, a court awarded her 2.3 million dollars. That same year, Connecticut passed the Family Violence Prevention and Response Act, which mandates that police arrest a perpetrator whenever there is probable cause that a family violence crime has been committed. According to a 2008 report from the National Institute of Justice, twenty-three states had passed legislation mandating that arrest be made for family violence crimes.[53]

In 1994, the Violence Against Women Act (VAWA) was passed by Congress. The original intent was to raise awareness of domestic violence (DV), improve services for victims, enhance police and criminal court response to DV, and establish grant programs to target certain crimes, including IPV. Over the years Congress has reauthorized VAWA to broaden its protections and services for victims. Notably, only in the presence of physical violence or a threat of physical violence do our laws and court systems provide protection to victims of IPV. No legal protection is available to victims struggling with emotional abuse, unless that abuse includes threats of physical violence.

Societal attitudes and legal responses to IPV have no doubt greatly improved. Physical abuse of wives was simply not spoken

---

53   There is considerable research on whether mandatory arrest laws have been helpful to victims of IPV. In some states, both the victim and perpetrator have been arrested because the victim fought back, leaving evidence of an attack on the perpetrator. This is known as "dual arrest." The discussion of dual arrest, subsequent revisions to mandatory arrest laws, and whether mandatory arrest has been helpful to victims of IPV is beyond the scope of this chapter.

of, even though it was happening in the 1950s. Similarly, forcing a wife to have sex was just one of the things that could happen to a wife; now it is marital rape. Within the last seventy years progress has been made, but there is still more to do.

Frequency and Costs of IPV

Compiling statistics on the frequency and costs of IPV often can only be estimated because many incidents of IPV go unreported to police and medical providers. Statistics and rates can vary depending on the methods used to compile them. According to one 2011 report from the National Center for Injury Prevention and Control, in the United States more than one in three woman and one in four men have experienced rape, physical violence, and/or stalking by an intimate partner in their lifetimes. Almost half of all women have experienced psychological aggression by an intimate partner.

According to a 2001 report for the Bureau of Justice Statistics, 85 percent of those victimized by IPV were females. There is also some indication that since 1993 there has been a decrease in non-fatal violent crimes, perhaps due to publicity, shelters, treatment, and enhanced punishment of offenders. However, the severity of nonfatal violent crimes may be increasing. In 2008 the Bureau of Justice Statics reported that in 2007, an intimate partner committed three out of every four murders of women in the United States. Children often witness IPV, as four out of ten female victims of IPV live in households with children under twelve years of age. Women between the ages of 16 and 24 years have the highest rates of IPV victimization—19.7 out of 1,000, and only half of the incidents of IPV are reported to police.

The costs of IPV include the physical, emotional, and spiritual injury to victims, the loss of dignity and respect for victims and their abusive partners, and the monetary costs we as society bear. In 1990, the *Journal of the American Medical Association (JAMA)* reported that the leading cause of injury to women between the ages of 15 and 44 is IPV. These injuries exceed the number of women harmed by car accidents, muggings, and cancer deaths— combined. JAMA also reported that 20 percent of all women who visit an emergency room for treatment have been battered, and that between 22 to 57 percent of all homeless women reported some form of domestic violence as the immediate cause of their homelessness.

Nearly $37 billion is spent on law enforcement, legal work, medical care, and lost productivity due to family violence. It is estimated that U.S. employers lose $14 billion dollars annually due to absenteeism and lost productivity due to family violence. That is a loss of almost eight million days of work—more than 32,000 full-time jobs.[54]

The Role of Weapons in IPV

Almost any household object can become a weapon in the hands of an abusive partner. According to studies cited by Johns Hopkins School of Public Health, in the general population, the presence of a gun in a home increases the risk of homicide threefold; when the offender is an intimate partner, the risk of homicide increases eightfold; and the risk of being murdered with a gun increases twentyfold when there are previous incidents of IPV. Of all women killed by guns, two-thirds are killed by intimate partners. Abusive partners who use a weapon (a gun, a knife, or a vehicle) are more likely to perpetrate further acts of violence against a victim than abusive partners who do not use weapons.

To prevent abusive partners from having access to firearms, two categories of laws have been enacted: gun seizure laws and laws that prohibit gun purchases. These laws vary from state to state. Gun seizure laws generally give authority to police to seize any guns at the scene of a domestic violence call or in possession of an abusive partner. Similarly, judges are given the authority to order abusive partners to surrender their guns if a restraining order or protective order[55] is in effect. Prohibitions on the purchase of guns may apply to anyone convicted of a domestic violence crime or anyone subject to a restraining order or protective order.

According to the National Criminal Background Check System, during the four years from 1998 to 2001 there were two hundred thousand denials of requests for approval to purchase a gun. Of

---

54   A number of states now require employers to provide employees with *Family Violence Leave Time* to address safety issues, court appearances, or medical treatment related to family violence.

55   There are differences between Restraining Orders and Protective Orders. Those differences vary from state to state. Both are court orders that generally require an abusive partner to refrain from harassing, threatening, assaulting, or being within a certain distance of the victim. These orders can direct the abusive partner to vacate the home if the abusive partner and victim reside together. In some cases these orders can include conditions for temporary custody for children.

these, 14 percent were due to misdemeanor convictions related to domestic violence. During this time there were also three thousand referrals to the Bureau of Alcohol, Tobacco and Firearms for seizure of guns that had been sold to people who were ineligible to purchase firearms. These three thousand people had misdemeanor convictions for DV related crimes. They had been granted permission to purchase firearms only because the background check could not be completed within the legal time limit. During 2008 in the state of Connecticut, 14 percent of state applications for gun ownership were denied due to a conviction for a DV crime or issuance of a restraining order.

Guns are not the only cause of death of victims of IPV. In 2013 in the state of North Carolina, sixty-two people were murdered in some type of domestic violence crime. Of those sixty-two deaths, thirty-eight were caused by firearms, ten involved knives, and all remaining deaths were caused by stabbing, suffocation, strangulation, sharp objects, blunt force object, automobiles, or unknown causes. Between the years 2000 and 2011 there were 175 deaths related to IPV in the state of Connecticut. Of the 175 homicide victims, 153 were female and 22 were male. Of the perpetrators, 156 were male and 19 were female. In Connecticut the percentage of deaths caused by knives was close to that caused by guns: 36 percent were caused by knives and 38 percent were caused by guns.

Clearly there is an increased risk of serious injury or death for victims of IPV who live in homes with guns, or whose abusive partner has access to a gun. Removing guns from the environment will not eliminate all risk of death, but it can surely reduce such risk.

The Risks and Resources Unique to Each Victim

Each victim knows the risks s/he faces. The risks created by an abusive partner, such as hitting, punching, slapping, and emotional abuse can be exacerbated by circumstances and characteristics of the victim that are present with or without an abusive partner. Examples of these circumstances and characteristics include a lack of education or job experience, medical conditions, and racism or other forms of discrimination. Abusive partners can use these life circumstances to further their control of the victim, i.e., "You'll never get hired anywhere because you're too stupid to get a GED," or, "No one in this town will ever rent to your kind."

Each victim is unique with their own set of risks, some caused by the abusive partner and others due to life circumstances. Each victim has his or her own resources to draw on, both internal and external. No two victims have exactly the same set of risks and resources. Each victim naturally creates a safety plan to minimize risks of harm to herself and her children. This planning process can be enhanced with the assistance of an experienced DV advocate who can listen and reflect to the victim the plan the victim creates, helping to share possible resources that may minimize some of the risks. DV advocates do not tell victims what to do. Rather, they assist victims to create their own plans. The victim knows her risks and resources better than anyone else—even better than trained advocates.

All of us engage in some version of safety planning as we move through our lives. When walking to the car in a parking lot at night, the keys are in our hands before stepping into the dark. That is a safety plan that reduces risks. This is the same process that victims of IPV use. If a victim knows that her abusive partner is likely to be physically violent when drinking and watching football on the weekends, she might decide to go visit her mother for the weekend, or invite a sister to spend the weekend if she believes that the presence of another adult will deter his violent behavior. Victims know their risks better than anyone else—they will know best whether the presence of another will deter violence.

Some options available to victims of IPV are not helpful to all victims. Consider restraining orders: these are court orders that the victim applies for. The order can direct the abusive partner to stay away from the victim and may contain other provisions to enhance the victim's safety. If a victim believes that the abusive partner will respect the law and abide by a court order, seeking a restraining order is a good option to enhance safety. If, however, a victim feels that a restraining order will exacerbate violence that is already escalating, this is not a good option for this victim. A restraining order should not be a component of her safety plan. Only the victim knows how all the unique risks and resources in their particular situation play out.

Certain risk factors for IPV are more common. They include alcohol or substance abuse by a victim or abusive partner, children, work history and employment, the degree of isolation, rural settings, pregnancy, immigration status, sexual orientation, language, and whether the abusive partner is in law enforcement or the military. Authorities generally agree that the following are life-threatening risks: access to guns, past use of a weapon, threats with a weapon, threats to kill, serious injury in the past, threats of suicide, drug and/or alcohol abuse, forced sex and obsessiveness, extreme jealousy or dominance. These are some of the risks a victim takes into account when deciding whether to stay or leave the relationship.

Leaving an abusive relationship is one of the most dangerous things a victim can do. This is because IPV is a pattern of coercive control. If the victim leaves, the abusive partner's control diminishes. An abusive partner may do whatever is necessary to keep the victim in the relationship. Escalating threats and violence may occur. Moreover, leaving is not likely to eliminate many of the risks faced when in the relationship. Take money for example. If the victim stays in the relationship, the abusive partner will continue to have control over the victim's access to money. What happens to a victim's access for financial resources if she leaves? At least temporarily she may be in much worse financial shape than when in the relationship. Consider the risk of physical violence from an abusive partner. If a victim stays in the relationship, she is at risk and may have developed strategies to reduce this risk; if she leaves, the risk of physical violence may be exacerbated. Not only is leaving an abusive relationship dangerous, leaving does not eliminate all the risks associated with the abusive partner.

The most accurate indicators of a victim's risks from an abusive partner are the victim's perception and analysis of the danger.[56] From the outside, a situation may appear one way while the lived experience is quite different. This is not to say that all victims should stay in abusive relationships, but rather that for some victims, choosing to stay in the relationship for the time being is a rational decision—a decision to be respected.

Roles of the Church and the Challenges of Respecting the Dignity of Victims and Their Abusive Partners

It is impossible for Christians, individually or corporately as the Church, to live out our baptismal vows without engaging the issue

---

56 Advocates for victims try to engage in client-centered advocacy in which the decisions of clients are respected and honored, not supplanted by the advocate's views of the situation. In the face of a victim's significant mental illness or substance abuse, the victim's analysis may be impaired. In these cases an advocate may need to exercise more persuasion.

of IPV on some level. As human beings we prefer not to "see" violence and brokenness in our midst; it is easier and more comfortable to believe that this happens in other communities, not ours. If you believe this, you are likely mistaken. IPV is in our midst. The question is, what are you and your congregation going to do about it?

There are many ways individuals and congregations can address the brokenness that is inherent in IPV and support individual victims and abusive partners as they seek wholeness. Churches can become places where it is acceptable to talk about IPV. For many congregations, this may be a change in culture. To start, someone from the congregation, perhaps a parishioner, ordained leader, member of the vestry or pastoral care team, could contact your state's Domestic Violence Coalition; every state has one. Generally state coalitions receive federal funds and distribute them to shelter programs throughout the state. The DV shelters are members of the coalition.[57] Coalitions may have educational resources and publications printed and available to the public. Usually coalition websites contain a wealth of information.

There are two basic approaches parishes can take to engage IPV. The first is on a policy level. This generally involves advocacy on the local, state, and/or federal levels. The state DV coalition can provide guidance on how a church might be most effective in these efforts. Any lobbying efforts should be coordinated through the coalition. The other approach is to focus on individuals impacted by IPV. This focus on individuals could entail pastoral care and support to those impacted, connecting people to services already available in the community, or being a companion as an individual seeks to make changes in her life. Of these approaches, one is not better than the other—both are needed. How a congregation decides to engage IPV should be guided by the charisms of the congregation.

To increase awareness and promote conversation, a parish could hold an adult forum on IPV. Often coalitions have speakers available to come and address groups. Many coalitions and shelters have speakers who work with youth and address teen dating violence. This could be a facilitated conversation for a senior youth group. Another step a parish can take is to put resource cards for

---

57   Coalitions usually do not provide direct service to individual victims or abusive partners—that is the role of the shelter programs and education programs. The coalition's role is to coordinate policy advocacy (perhaps lobby at the state legislature for laws to improve the responses to IPV), ensure that fatality reviews are conduced and publicized, and provide information to the public.

victims of IPV in all women's restrooms at church.[58] These cards are the size of a traditional business card so that victims can take them discretely; they may have screening questions to help people identify if they are in an abusive relationship and offer hotline phone numbers that are answered 24/7/365.

The groups or individuals who are heading up this effort in the congregation should know how to contact the local DV shelter and be familiar with all the services offered through that shelter. Often people assume that shelters only shelter those who are leaving abusive relationships. Generally shelters provide a wide array of services to victims staying in the relationships as well as those leaving. Shelters will often run facilitated off-site support groups for victims. Groups are often single gender groups. Some shelters will offer programs for children who have lived with or are living with IPV in their homes.[59] Some of these programs are for mothers and their children. There are also programs to enhance the parenting skills of those who have been victimized by IPV.

Offering pastoral care and support to a victim of IPV can be challenging. One of the hardest aspects can be to respect the victim's dignity by respecting and honoring decisions the victim makes, even when you believe that is not the best decision. Often victims of IPV are emotionally worn down. They have lost control over many aspects of their lives. It is healing and affirming for the victim to be in control of decisions they are now making. The role of the pastoral caregiver is to receive what the victim offers; to listen and assure the victim she is not alone. This has happened to many others. Be present to the victim, and pray with and for the victim and all involved. A pastoral care provider should refrain from jumping in and trying to fix the situation for the victim (unless the victim asks you to), imposing their own judgment, blaming and shaming the victim for choosing to stay in the relationship or taking so long to leave. The pastoral care provider should also refrain from weighing the risks the victim faces—this work, which is safety planning, is best done by trained DV advocates. Advocates are available by phone by calling a local or national hotline number. The care provider could support the victim by being present, if the victim wishes, during this phone conversation.

---

58 Appropriately worded resource cards could of course be provided in men's restrooms.

59 Children who witness IPV are harmed, even if the child is not physically injured. Witnessing IPV as a child raises questions regarding the legal obligation of reporting suspected abuse or neglect of children to state child protective services. These issues regarding mandated reporting are beyond the scope of this essay.

If a pastoral care provider tries to impose their ideas on the victim, the victim may decide not to have further conversations with the care provider. Victims already have challenging lives—they are not likely to spend time on efforts they feel are not helpful to their situation, or make them feel worse about themselves than they already do. Care providers and the Church need to stay relevant in the lives of victims; without being in their lives, the Good News of Christ cannot be brought to them.

It is helpful to victims if the pastoral care provider acknowledges the violence, focuses on empowerment by affirming those aspects of the victim's life she is taking control of, is part of a support network, and can act as a referral resource. Pastoral care providers should be aware that although couples' counseling can be helpful in many situations, it is not helpful in the face of IPV due to the significant imbalance of power. The impact of suggesting couples' counseling to the victim can feel as though the care provider is dismissing concerns about safety by telling the victim to go back to the abusive partner and work it out in counseling. Moreover, the risk of violence may escalate if the abusive partner learns that the victim is talking to anyone about the violence.

Serving as a companion or pastoral care provider to an abusive partner also has its challenges. Often when we think about IPV or DV, we think about the harm to the victim and children. We don't automatically think about the impact this has on the abusive partner. While the abusive partner's behavior may be abhorrent, the abusive partner is, like each of us, a child of God for whom Christ died on the cross. The abusive behavior comes from a place of brokenness. Individuals who know the love of God have moments of frustration when they act in less than charitable ways toward loved ones, but do not engage in ongoing patterns of coercive control of a loved one through physical, sexual, and/or emotional abuse.

Abusive partners are in pain, whether or not they are able to admit this to themselves or others. Bravado may be masking fear, insecurity, or feelings of inadequacy. Some abusive partners have a deep fear of abandonment; this fear can contribute to a need to control their intimate partner to prevent that partner from leaving. In essence, such abusive partners use violence to try to prevent this fear from becoming a reality. No degree of underlying pain justifies or excuses abusive behavior. Recognizing the presence of underlying pain may help us to find our common humanity with abusive partners. As victims face risks from IPV, so too do their abusive partners—they face the risk of criminal prosecution, imprisonment; loss of reputation, employment, and income. More-over, they risk the loss of relationships with children and the inti-mate partner they are abusing.

Pastoral care providers can be a source of support to abusive partners as they seek to amend their behaviors and find new ways of being in relationship. Ideally, pastoral care providers can refer abusive partners to resources such as support groups or education programs that focus on family violence. Unfortunately, there aren't many such programs and those that do exist are often connected with the court system. In some locations, the only way to access these programs is through a court order.[60]

Pastoral care providers can be companions to abusive partners; they can be there to listen to abusive partners who may be frus-trated with court proceedings or their intimate partners. Supporting abusive partners in efforts to comply with any type of court order is helpful to the abusive partner as well as the victim. Sometimes a pastoral care provider may be able to help an abusive partner develop a plan for those times when the partner feels frustrated, angry, or a loss of control that can lead to IPV. Identifying unac-ceptable behaviors, being clear that the behavior is unacceptable for any reason, and exploring ways to reduce the likelihood of future violent behavior is a component of pastoral care. While at times it may feel confrontational, helping to stop someone from engaging in violent behavior is a form of pastoral care.

Our hope, and the hopes of victims of IPV, is that abusive part-ners will change their behaviors and stop being violent. Attempting to change one's own behavior, recognizing hurt caused by past behaviors, and amending one's life, is hard work. Amendment of life is even more difficult when one is feeling blamed, shamed, or isolated. As Christians, we believe that all can be redeemed through Christ. Seeking ways to support abusive partners as they work to amend their lives, while challenging, is work we are called to do.

Questions may arise as to whether those who provide pastoral care to victims and/or abusive partners should accompany vic-tims and/or abusive partners to court, and if so, what their role should be at the courthouse. Anyone who has been to court for any

---

60   This is potentially an area in which policy advocacy could be fruitful—to create
     additional resources to help abusive partners change their behaviors. However, with
     limited public resources, allocating further resources for such efforts may reduce
     resources available to victims of IPV. Moreover, absent court involvement, many
     abusive partners are not motivated to recognize the need to change their behaviors or
     face the underlying pain.

reason knows that there can be long hours of waiting. In matters pertaining to IPV, there often can be anxiety and fear on the part of both victims and abusive partners. Having a companion to sit and pray with can be comforting and may lessen anxiety, which can improve decision-making and judgment.

A particular challenge can arise when both partners are members of the congregation, or when both have received pastoral care from the parish priest over the years. In such cases clergy and laity providing pastoral care need to proceed carefully to avoid the appearance of, or actually taking sides against a member or parishioner. While we are called to speak the truth and confront unacceptable behavior, we are also called not to abandon anyone, even sinners.

All care providers to individuals impacted by IPV need to set boundaries for themselves. First and foremost, they need to be aware of the limits of their expertise. It is one thing to be a sounding board and companion to an abusive partner, it is quite another and unacceptable to try to set up conversations with the victim and abusive partner—even if this is what the abusive partner says is necessary to move forward.[61] Second, and equally important, is that care providers need an appropriate confidential place to debrief, perhaps with a pastor, therapist, or spiritual advisor.

Our culture's response to IPV has come a long way in the last sixty years. There is still much to be done. While we may not want to believe or see that IPV is present in almost all walks of life, it is. It is, in our congregations and beyond. To bring the Good News of Christ to others, and respect the dignity of every human being, as we covenant to do with God's help, we must be aware of and willing to address IPV. There are opportunities for congregations both to partner with other organizations to do this work from a policy perspective, and to focus on supporting individual victims and their abusive partners.

———

Robin Hammeal-Urban, J.D., is canon for Mission Integrity and Training for the Episcopal Church in Connecticut and has worked with numerous congregations following the misconduct of trusted

---

61   While a victim's risk analysis is to be respected and trusted, this is not true of the abusive partner's assessment of the situation. The abusive partner has already been violent, manipulative, and secretive—all aspects of IPV.

leaders. From 1985 to 2002 she served as an attorney with Greater Hartford Legal Aid in the area of outreach and policy with the New England Network on Domestic Violence and Poverty. This essay is based on a workshop she presented at "Reclaiming the Gospel of Peace."

For Reflection

1. Where is your story in this story?
2. Where do you see God?
3. What causes you to pause and rethink your previous assumptions?
4. What cries out to you?
5. What calls to you?

Go Deeper

1. Do you know your local 800-number for IPV reporting and support?
2. Where are the local DV centers in your community? How can you (or your congregation) support their ministry?
3. What steps might you (or your congregation) take to provide support and resources to those affected by IPV who attend worship and church functions?
4. What training is provided to those who offer pastoral care in your congregation?
5. What training is offered to members of your congregation regarding the awareness of misconduct and abuse? How might this become more visible to all your members?

20

Talking Peace: Learning and Telling Biblical Stories of Peace

Dina McMullin Ferguson

If we are to reclaim the Gospel of Peace, there has to be a Gospel of Peace that can be claimed. And we need to share and tell these stories of peace to our children, and all who have ears to hear. The dramatic bookends of our scriptural tradition—Genesis and Revelation—tell us that God created us in peace and for peace, and that ultimately we will dwell with God in peace. The world begins and ends with remarkable stories of peace.

> *In the beginning when God created the heavens and the earth, the earth was a formless void and darkness covered the face of the deep, while a wind from God swept over the face of the waters. Then God said, "Let there be light"; and there was light.* (Genesis 1:1-3)

The world is spoken into existence by performative speech and then consistently and repeatedly declared good. As the Hebrew says, *"Tov. Ke Tov."*

This is in contrast with a number of creation stories from other traditions. The Babylonian creation story, the Enuma Elish, tells of the violent dismemberment of the goddess of chaos, Tiamat, by Marduk for the creation of the earth and sky. In the second creation story found in Genesis (2:4b–25), Elohim lovingly forms the human creature from the earth. And to satisfy the need for a helpmate, the creature is put to sleep before being separated into male and female humans. Creation in Genesis is good and created peacefully.

The Revelation of John is interpreted by some contemporary biblical scholars as the reconception of warfare as spiritual conflict between the angels of God and the angels of the enemy in which the role of the believers is nonviolent resistance as modeled by the Lamb at the right hand of God.[62] Revelation projects the end-time battle on a cosmic scale with the powers of good and evil facing one another. The central theme is that through Christ the Lord, God will totally defeat all enemies and humanity will finally dwell with God in peace. The ending is a victory of peace in the New Jerusalem.

So the Bible begins in peace and order and ends in peace and rejoicing. But in between . . . where and what is this Gospel of Peace?

Within Holy Scripture are many stories of war and conflict. But they are surrounded by and include stories of peace. Peace is more than the absence of war or the cessation of hostilities. The Hebrew word "shalom" incorporates the concepts of completeness and wholeness, which can be found throughout the stories of our faith. These stories choose peace over war, reconciliation over retribution, inclusion over exclusion and scapegoating, and crossing boundaries rather than remaining insular.

One of the first stories of peace and reconciliation involves Jacob and Esau, two brothers in conflict. You may remember that Esau sold his birthright for a mess of pottage and was tricked out of his blessing by his mother, Rebekah, and brother, Jacob. At the end of this story, Esau is murderously furious (Genesis 27:41) and Jacob flees for his life. Years later, when Jacob is told by God to return to his own country from Midian, he is in dread of meeting Esau:

> And Jacob said, "O God of my father Abraham and God of my father Isaac, O Lord who said to me, 'Return to your country and to your kindred, and I will do you good,' I am not worthy of the least of all the steadfast love and all the faithfulness that you have shown to your servant, for with only my staff I crossed this Jordan; and now I have become

---

62   Thomas E. Boomershine, PhD, in telephone conversation, September 2013.

two companies. Deliver me, please, from the hand of my brother, from the hand of Esau, for I am afraid of him; he may come and kill us all, the mothers with the children. Yet you have said, 'I will surely do you good, and make your offspring as the sand of the sea, which cannot be counted because of their number.'" (Genesis 32:9–12)

In the Jacob and Esau tradition, the story that we tend to forget is this one of reconciliation. At the end of the story, when Jacob is terrified of Esau coming with his army of four hundred men, there is unexpected and generous reconciliation.

Now Jacob looked up and saw Esau coming, and four hundred men with him. So he divided the children among Leah and Rachel and the two maids. He put the maids with their children in front, then Leah with her children, and Rachel and Joseph last of all. He himself went on ahead of them, bowing himself to the ground seven times, until he came near his brother. But Esau ran to meet him, and embraced him, and fell on his neck and kissed him, and they wept. (Genesis 33:1–4)

There is no denying that the stories in the Hebrew Scriptures continue to overwhelm with violence. It is difficult to see stories of peace in the midst of the rumors and details of wars. But there is a tradition of peace, especially in the stories of Elijah and Elisha doing good to their enemies: the widow of Zarephath (1 Kings 17:7–16), the Shunnamite woman (2 Kings 4:8–37), and the healing of Naaman (2 Kings 5:1–19), the general of the Syrian army that invaded and eventually conquered the northern kingdom of Israel. One particular story, Elisha and the army of Aram, is a small gem of intentional peacemaking:

Once when the king of Aram was at war with Israel, he took counsel with his officers. He said, "At such and such a place shall be my camp." But the man of God sent word to the king of Israel, "Take care not to pass this place, because the Arameans are going down there." The king of Israel sent word to the place of which the man of God spoke. More than once or twice he warned such a place so that it was on the alert.

The mind of the king of Aram was greatly perturbed because of this; he called his officers and said to them,

*"Now tell me who among us sides with the king of Israel?"
Then one of his officers said, "No one, my lord king. It is
Elisha, the prophet in Israel, who tells the king of Israel
the words that you speak in your bedchamber." He said,
"Go and find where he is; I will send and seize him." He
was told, "He is in Dothan." So he sent horses and chariots there and a great army; they came by night, and surrounded the city.*

*When an attendant of the man of God rose early in the
morning and went out, an army with horses and chariots
was all around the city. His servant said, "Alas, master!
What shall we do?" He replied, "Do not be afraid, for there
are more with us than there are with them." Then Elisha
prayed: "O Lord, please open his eyes that he may see." So
the Lord opened the eyes of the servant, and he saw; the
mountain was full of horses and chariots of fire all around
Elisha. When the Arameans came down against him, Elisha
prayed to the Lord, and said, "Strike this people, please,
with blindness." So he struck them with blindness as Elisha
had asked. Elisha said to them, "This is not the way, and
this is not the city; follow me, and I will bring you to the
man whom you seek." And he led them to Samaria.*

*As soon as they entered Samaria, Elisha said, "O Lord,
open the eyes of these men so that they may see." The
Lord opened their eyes, and they saw that they were inside
Samaria. When the king of Israel saw them he said to
Elisha, "Father, shall I kill them? Shall I kill them?" He
answered, "No! Did you capture with your sword and your
bow those whom you want to kill? Set food and water before
them so that they may eat and drink; and let them go to
their master." So he prepared for them a great feast; after
they ate and drank, he sent them on their way, and they
went to their master. And the Arameans no longer came
raiding into the land of Israel.* (2 Kings 6:8–23)

Unfortunately, these events do not exert peaceful influences
on the king of Israel. After this series of peacemaking stories, the
rest of 2 Kings is about the various wars that end in the disaster
of the Babylonian conquest and Zedekiah's misplaced faith that
God would deliver them if they faithfully defied the Babylonians.
But the great prophet Jeremiah is in the background of that
entire story. He constantly advocated surrender and nonviolent
resistance.

This tells us something. Israel did not follow the way of peace—and it cost them. The northern kingdom was totally lost to Assyria and in the south, Judah suffered the Babylonian exile.

Consider this quote, "Because the stories we tell determine what we think about what happens, which determines what happens next."[63] There is no objective history; interpretation of events is determinative. It is how we interpret events—the stories we tell about the events—that define them for us and determine how we react to them.

Recent scholarship identifies the final editing of the Hebrew Scriptures to have been done in the wake of the Babylonian exile. The devastation of war resulted in editorial choices in the Old Testament showing that the way of violence and war was disastrous for Israel. This is the story the Hebrew people were telling themselves in the wake of the exile. And this is the tradition from which Jesus emerges.

Jesus comes out of a tradition that knows the cost of war and sees the current situation in which he lives as a dangerous and disastrous analog to that tradition. The Zealots who are in the midst of Israel at the time of Jesus are part of the tradition of attempting violent overthrow of their oppressors—this time the Romans. Jesus knows the cost of following the tradition of violence as opposed to the way of peace.

> *"Teacher, which commandment in the law is the greatest?" He said to him, "'You shall love the Lord your God with all your heart, and with all your soul, and with all your mind.' This is the greatest and first commandment. And a second is like it: 'You shall love your neighbor as yourself.' On these two commandments hang all the law and the prophets."* (Matthew 22:36–40)

Jesus is at odds with the Jewish leaders and we see how he is continuing the prophetic ministry of Elisha with many acts of reconciliation, crossing boundaries, and including the outcast. Many of Jesus's healings are specifically of Gentiles, people who were Israel's enemies, notably: healing the Gerasene demoniac (Luke 8:26–39), the Syrophoenician woman (Mark 7:24–30), curing the deaf man in the region of Decapolis (Mark 7:31–37), the feeding of the four thousand (Mark 8:1–9), and curing the blind man at Bethsaida (Mark 8:22–26).

---

63   Katie Orenstein, founder and CEO of the Op-Ed Project.

The story of Bartimaeus is an example of Jesus crossing boundaries to include the bullied and outcast:

> *They came to Jericho. As he and his disciples and a large crowd were leaving Jericho, Bartimaeus son of Timaeus, a blind beggar, was sitting by the roadside. When he heard that it was Jesus of Nazareth, he began to shout out and say, "Jesus, Son of David, have mercy on me!" Many sternly ordered him to be quiet, but he cried out even more loudly, "Son of David, have mercy on me!" Jesus stood still and said, "Call him here." And they called the blind man, saying to him, "Take heart; get up, he is calling you." So throwing off his cloak, he sprang up and came to Jesus. Then Jesus said to him, "What do you want me to do for you?" The blind man said to him, "My teacher, let me see again." Jesus said to him, "Go; your faith has made you well." Immediately he regained his sight and followed him on the way.* (Mark 10:46–52)

As part of the Gospel of Peace, it is important to note that the original telling of these stories as they come to us in the Gospel of Mark is in the decades after the Jewish-Roman war and the destruction of the Second Temple (70 CE). In this setting the original audience hears a Gospel of Peace rather than a gospel of violence, retribution, and war. We are invited to hear this gospel as well.

Throughout his ministry, Jesus attacked the powers of evil by doing good; he never hurts another person—pigs seem to be the only ones affected negatively by his life and work. The stories of Jesus's conflict with the Pharisees and scribes can be heard as stories of real encounters and dialogue with other serious students of the law. It is nonviolent engagement. This includes Judas Iscariot, who betrays him in the passion narrative. In the Synoptics, Jesus shares bread and wine, his body and blood, with Judas. The entire narrative of Jesus's passion and death is an example of nonviolent resistance and a radically different model of how the Messiah will save the people. An important theme in the passion story can be seen as a choice between Barabbas, a Zealot, and Jesus, the Messiah of peace (Mark 15:6–15; Matthew 27:15–23).

Martin Luther King Jr. is a contemporary example of Jesus as the way of peace. "Nonviolence means avoiding not only external physical violence but also internal violence of the spirit. You not only refuse to shoot a man, but you refuse to hate him."[64] After Jesus's death and resurrection, the way of peace became foundational for the church. The story of Peter and Cornelius, a centurion in the Roman army, is told twice—first as it happens in Acts 10 and then as Peter reports the story to the apostles and believers in Acts 11. This repetition (the only example in the Bible of a story being told twice in succession) establishes the importance of this story for the formation and theology of the early Christian community.

> *Then Peter began to speak to them: "I truly understand that God shows no partiality, but in every nation anyone who fears him and does what is right is acceptable to him. You know the message he sent to the people of Israel, preaching peace by Jesus Christ—he is Lord of all.* (Acts 10:34–36)

Reclaiming the Gospel of Peace is something that has been done over the centuries. At the turn of the fifth century, Moses the Black was convicted by the Gospel of Peace and changed his life from one of violence and carousing to one of compassion and peace. Early church historian Samilinius Sozomen wrote of Moses the Black that "no one else ever made such a change from evil to excellence." Moses is a shining example of the transformative power of the gospel. He is the patron saint of nonviolence.

> God of transforming power and transfiguring mercy: Listen to the prayers of all who, like Abba Moses, cry to you: "O God whom we do not know, let us know you!" Draw them and all of us from unbelief to faith and from violence into your peace, through the cross of Jesus our Savior; who lives and reigns with you, in the unity of the Holy Spirit, one God, now and forever. Amen.[65]

The Gospel of Peace continues to require reclaiming. We need to know the stories, learn the stories, and tell the stories of peace. Let us be about the work of Jesus's Gospel of Peace.

---

64   Martin Luther King Jr., *A Testament of Hope: The Essential Writings and Speeches of Martin Luther King, Jr.*, ed. James M. Washington (San Francisco: HarperOne, 2003), 313.

65   Collect for Moses the Black. *Holy Women, Holy Men* (New York: Church Pension Group, 2010), 547.

The Reverend Dina McMullin Ferguson, DMin., is an Episcopal priest in the Diocese of Los Angeles and past president of the Network of Biblical Storytellers. Her interest is in proclaiming the Scriptures in the oral tradition: in order to reclaim the Gospel of Peace, we must first know and claim the Gospel of Peace.

For Reflection

1. Where is your story in this story?
2. Where do you see God?
3. What causes you to pause and rethink your previous assumptions?
4. What cries out to you?
5. What calls to you?

Go Deeper

1. What other stories do you know in which the characters choose peace over violence?
2. How might sharing these biblical stories with children reshape their understanding and flicker their imaginations about the Gospel of Peace?

21

Holy Conversations

Kay Collier McLaughlin

It seems impossible to escape the violence that is pervading our country and our world. Before I left my home in Kentucky to attend this conference on "Reclaiming the Gospel of Peace," a shooting took place not far from my office, taking the lives of four people. The TV in the Chicago airport was reporting another school shooting—and here we are in Oklahoma City, the site of one of the most tragic and unforgettable acts of violence this country has ever known. Before we finish grieving one incident, another follows on its heels.

Before we can begin to address how to *end* violence, however, I believe we have to address how it *begins*. Not *out there*, but inside ourselves, in our own hearts, minds, and souls. With how people of all ages, in all places, at all times, handle differences: differences of experience, differences of opinions, and differences of backgrounds, ethnicity, and gender.

We have become a people without respect for each other, which means we do not listen to each other. We do not know *how* to listen or to speak when we are not of the same mind on a given subject or event, and so we allow our reactions to what is unfamiliar or different from our experience and opinion to escalate into talking about rather than directly to individuals, emotional reactivity rather than reasoned response, escalation of differences and mean-spiritedness that can lead to emotional, spiritual, and physical violence.

It would be easy to say it happens "out there" across the world, in places other than our homes and neighborhoods and certainly in places other than our churches. But the truth is that we cannot point our fingers at the culture and act as if the influence of the culture is seeping into our churches like poison gas when the same attitudes and behaviors we claim that we abhor march right with us into our pews.

The hard truth is that violence begins within each of us—within you and within me—with attitudes and behaviors of disrespect that have nothing to do with the Baptismal Covenant to respect the dignity of every human being. It has everything to do with our unwillingness, or simply our unconsciousness, about the need to examine our own blind and dark places that allow the roots of violence to lay in wait within us.

Sadly, these attitudes and behaviors have become so normative that we do not even blink an eye when they happen in front of us, or within us.

And the change—the end to the violence—has to begin within the individual, within each of us—you and me. I have to acknowledge my own tendencies to reactive thoughts, feelings, and behaviors and become intentional in choosing another way of being and doing in the world.

In the Diocese of Lexington, our efforts at changing these attitudes and behaviors are called "Holy Conversations." At the heart of our process are the African words—"Suwa Bona"—"I see you, I hear you." What we have learned from our African brothers and sisters is that these words have a far deeper meaning than we might think. What they are saying is that unless I *truly* see, *truly* hear another person with my full attention, my full ability to listen and honor the truth of what they are telling me of their experience, I am in essence saying, "You do not exist; what you have experienced is unimportant to me; it does not matter. You do not matter."

The premise behind Holy Conversations is the desire to honor the existence and experience of the other in order to learn to live and work together in a healthy way. In Holy Conversations we acknowledge that often the things that divide us are the things about which we are most passionate, with a passion born in differing experiences and honed in different perspectives; we may have been hurt or believe we have been treated unfairly again and again, and no one cares, no one wants to hear our pain.

The process of Holy Conversations begins with individuals who are willing to become self-aware in order to become other aware, and the development of a process of respectful listening to each others' stories that allows us to engage any content or degree of difference without feeling violated or unheard, or resorting to demeaning, hurtful, or violent behaviors.

The process involves practices of

- Truthful naming of issues and positions
- Direct communication
- Respectful listening
- Regard for the life truth of others

The goal is not agreement, but the ability to live and work together in a healthy manner with the inevitable differences of experience and personality that come with the privilege of having been created as unique beings by an awesome God. If we are to be the countercultural entity we profess to be, we MUST begin with ourselves, and become intentional about carrying attitudes and practices of respectful, peaceful interaction into every part of our individual lives and worlds, modeling a different way of being.

Many outstanding theologians and teachers have spoken or written brilliantly on the need for civil dialogue and encounter in our culture. Such words are inspirational, but with a few exceptions, do not lead to *behavioral change.* The practice of an interactive process such as Holy Conversations offers the beginning of integration of the possibility of change behavior for individuals and systems.

It will not be easy. It is not easy. But in our work with the process known as Holy Conversations, we have experienced hope emerging from brokenness as individuals and organizations have learned that there is a way to live and work together that can build on differences rather than allow differences to lead to lack of civility and violence. What has been successfully implemented at a diocesan level is now being expanded to address a serious issue that impacts our world. Based on our assessment, such transformative opportunities are desired by many groups, yet efforts to offer them have been stymied by a sense that the problem is too large to approach.

We believe that extending a successful process throughout the church and beyond the Church through education can bring, as Margaret Wheatley says in her book *Turning To One Another: Restoring Hope for the Future,* real hope by offering a model that can be replicated in both faith-based and non-faith-based systems.

The time to begin is now. We invite you to join us.

Kay Collier McLaughlin, PhD, is a church professional of forty years standing, presently serving as the deputy for Leadership Development and Transition Ministries in the Diocese of Lexington (Kentucky). She travels extensively throughout the Episcopal Church (and beyond) giving workshops and consultations. This essay was part of her participation in a panel discussion on addressing violence in our communities at the "Reclaiming the Gospel of Peace" conference.

For Reflection

1. Where is your story in this story?
2. Where do you see God?
3. What causes you to pause and rethink your previous assumptions?
4. What cries out to you?
5. What calls to you?

Go Deeper

1. How do you handle violence within yourself—your heart, mind, and soul?
2. Where are the blind and dark places that may allow the roots of violence to take hold within you?
3. What Holy Conversations have you had?
4. What Holy Conversations do you wish you could have?
5. How might your congregation become a safe place to offer Holy Conversations?

The Episcopal Church's Legislative Response

Throughout its history, the Episcopal Church has taken a stand on numerous issues through its legislative process, either at its triennial General Convention or at Executive Council meetings between Conventions. Such resolutions often express the "mind" of the body as well as call upon dioceses, congregations, and individuals to act. What follows are the most recent pieces of legislation that have been approved in relation to gun violence:

"Responses to Gun Violence"

Resolved, That the Executive Council of The Episcopal Church, meeting in Linthicum Heights, Maryland, on February 27, 2013, express profound sorrow at the epidemic of gun violence in our communities, and urge Episcopalians to work toward comprehensive social responses that seek to stem the cycles of violence that fuel gun crime; and be it further

Resolved, That the Executive Council reaffirm General Convention Resolution 2000-D004 expressing "deep concern about the repeated use of easily available handguns and assault weapons by and against children, and call upon Episcopalians to seek ways to develop community strategies and create sanctuaries for our children, so that all may come to identify and value themselves and others as the precious children of God that they are, and that they may come to know peace in their lives and to create peace for future generations"; and be it further

Resolved, That the Executive Council reaffirm General Convention Resolution 1991-D088 calling the Episcopal Church to advocate for "public policy and adequate funding to provide comprehensive community-based services, hospital care and research into the causes and treatment of mental illness"; and emphasizes that mental-health services should be available and accessible without stigma in a variety of settings, including those who have suffered trauma from exposure to violence or violent environments; and be it further

Resolved, That the Executive Council support public-policy initiatives, such as the bipartisan "Excellence in Mental Health Care Act" pending in the United States Congress that seek to allow community-based mental healthcare providers the same opportunities to access federal funding as are currently allowed to providers of physical healthcare; and be it further

Resolved, That the Executive Council reaffirm General Convention Resolution 1997-C035 urging restrictions on the sale, ownership and use of firearms, particularly those that are easily concealable; and the enactment of tighter restrictions on the carrying of concealed weapons; and be it further

Resolved, That the Executive Council reaffirm General Convention Resolution 2000-B007 acknowledging that violence in our communities is encouraged and enabled by the presence of guns and calling for Episcopalians to advocate for the removal of handguns and assault weapons from our homes, communities and vehicles; and be it further

Resolved, That the Executive Council urge our elected officials to enact a clear and effective statute making gun trafficking a federal crime and empower law enforcement officials to investigate and prosecute straw purchasers, gun traffickers, and their entire criminal networks; and be it further

Resolved, That the Executive Council urge Episcopalians to examine our own cultural attitudes toward violence through efforts in our own congregations and communities, to repent of our own roles in the glorification and trivialization of violence, and to commit ourselves to another way.

EXPLANATION

On February 12, 2013, Presiding Bishop Katharine Jefferts Schori gave written testimony to the United States Senate Judiciary Subcommittee on the Constitution, Civil Rights and Human Rights, chaired by Senator Dick Durbin of Illinois, for the hearing on "Proposals to reduce gun violence: protecting our communities while respecting the Second Amendment."

In Presiding Bishop Jefferts Schori's written testimony, she summarizes the issue of gun violence in the United States, when she said:

> The United States has witnessed far too many public shootings in recent months and years. Far too many lives have been cut short or maimed by both random and targeted acts of gun violence. The school shooting in Newtown, CT, horrified Americans and people around the world, yet since that day several times as many young people have died by gunshot. Each year, gun violence claims the lives of more than three thousand children in the United States. The victims of each of these shootings are members of our families, religious congregations, and communities, and we continue to grieve for the living as well as the dead. . . ..
>
> This is no easy task. Just as the root causes of cyclical violence in our culture, and the ways in which that violence is expressed, are varied and complicated, so too are the solutions. We must resist the temptation to use the present moment of national angst as a pretext for preformed political agendas or simplistic responses that are better suited for sound bites than for meaningful, long-term change. We all share a responsibility to examine the many facets of cycles of violence in our society, and to discern equally comprehensive responses that will address the causes, means, and effects of violence.

The Episcopal Church has consistently been a voice of concern about gun violence and the exacerbation of violence wrought by easily available handguns and assault weapons, and a voice of support for making community-based mental health services readily available and accessible without stigma, as stated in the General Convention resolutions cited in this resolution and reprinted further in this Explanation.

"The Excellence in Mental Health Act" was introduced in the 113th Congress in early February by a bipartisan group of senators and representatives led by Senator Debbie Stabenow (D-MI) and Congressman Roy Blunt (R-MO). The Act strengthens community behavioral health centers that include mental health services, including 24-hour crisis care, integrated physical-mental-substance abuse treatment, and additional support for families of individuals living with mental health issues. The Act also establishes stringent quality standards and clinical outcome reporting measures, as well as authorizing Medicaid payment reforms that will strengthen the safety net to meet the mental health needs of returning veterans and the Affordable Care Act's insurance coverage expansions.

View the text of **S. 2257** (https://www.govtrack.us/congress/bills/113/s2257) and **H.R. 5989** (https://www.govtrack.us/congress/bills/112/hr5989), which are the same bills from the 112th Congress that did not make it out of their respective committees for a vote. The text of the current bills has not yet been posted to the Library of Congress site.

Below is the text of the General Convention resolutions cited in this resolution:

> **Resolution 2000-D004**: Express Concern About Availability of Handguns and Assault Weapons
> *Resolved*, That the 73rd General Convention express deep concern about the repeated use of easily available handguns and assault weapons by and against children and call upon Episcopalians to seek ways to develop community strategies and create sanctuaries for our children, so that all may come to identify and value themselves and others as the precious children of God that they are, and that they may come to know peace in their lives and to create peace for future generations.
>
> **Resolution 1991-D088**: Encourage Understanding of Mental Illness and Respond to the Needs of the Mentally Ill
> *Resolved*, the House of Deputies concurring, That members of the Episcopal Church are encouraged to become knowledgeable about mental illness in order to reduce stigma and stereotypes which are prevalent within the Church body and the Community-at-large; and be it further
> *Resolved*, That the Episcopal Church and all its units and organizations, be encouraged to reach out, welcome, include and support persons with a mental illness, particularly those

who have a prolonged, serious mental illness, and the families of those persons, and recognize the abilities and celebrate the gifts of those who have a mental illness; and be it further

Resolved, That the church encourage the development of specific programs to equip the clergy and laity for ministry to the mentally ill and their families and that clergy and lay ministers seek out training and opportunities to minister to the spiritual needs of those who are affected by a mental illness; and be it further

Resolved, That dioceses and congregations work with existing agencies and organizations to assist with and initiate programs, such as support groups, drop-in centers, housing and employment opportunities, which lead to an improved quality of life for people who have a mental illness, with specific attention to those who have become homeless; and be it further

Resolved, That dioceses, congregations and individual parishioners become advocates for public policy and adequate funding to provide comprehensive community-based services, hospital care and research into the causes and treatment of mental illness; and be it further

Resolved, That dioceses, congregations and individuals utilize the resources and support services offered by the Episcopal Mental Illness Network (EMIN) of the Presiding Bishop's Task Force on Accessibility.

Resolution 1997-C035: Urge Restrictions on Sale, Ownership and Use of Firearms

Resolved, That this 72nd General Convention, through the Office of Government Relations, urge the Congress of the Unites States to increase restrictions on the sale, ownership and use of firearms, particularly "Saturday night specials" (described as short-barreled, four inches or shorter, easily concealed handgun); and be it further

Resolved, That legislation to ban carrying concealed firearms be encouraged; and be it further

Resolved, That Congress be urged to adopt legislation requiring the Bureau of Alcohol, Tobacco and Firearms to develop regulations to delineate appropriate safety standards for use of firearms, and circumstances under which firearms may be used and to monitor and enforce compliance with said safety standards.

Resolution 2000-B007: Request the Removal of Handguns and Assault Weapons

Resolved, That the 73rd General Convention request members of the Episcopal Church of the United States of America to acknowledge that the violence in our communities is encouraged and enabled by the presence of guns; and be it further

Resolved, That this Convention call upon all members of the church to work intentionally in their several committees, legislatures, and institutions toward the removal of handguns and assault weapons from our homes, other residential communities, and vehicles.

For Reflection

1. Where is your story in this story?
2. Where do you see God?
3. What causes you to pause and rethink your previous assumptions?
4. What cries out to you?
5. What calls to you?

Go Deeper

1. Are you (or your congregation) involved in social justice issues? If so, how? If not, why not?
2. What ways can you share these pieces of legislation to your congregation?
3. How might your congregation adopt such resolutions?
4. What are ways to put this legislation into action more than words?

PeaceMeals: Connecting with Gun Shops

Bill Exner

St. Matthew's Episcopal Church in Goffstown, New Hampshire, is a chapter member of the Episcopal Peace Network. Their group, called "PeaceMeals," is all about building personal nonviolence skills, enjoying good company, and taking nonviolent action for peace and justice locally. Spurred by the increase of gun violence in their region, we did a little research and discovered this:

- Gun violence in the United States today accounts for eighty deaths daily of which ten are children.
- The youth rate of death by guns is twelve times higher in the United States than any other industrialized country.
- Seventy percent of the U.S. population favors more reasonable guidelines for gun ownership.
- Many weapons used in violent crimes in Massachusetts come from New Hampshire.
- Since 1933 more Americans have died from local gun violence than in all wars combined.

With this knowledge, PeaceMeals participants covenanted to:

1. Research gun dealers or sellers within a ten-mile radius of Goffstown. We expected to find one or two, but discovered there are fourteen, counting "antique" gun sellers.

2. We split up the list and agreed to contact each seller; two of us at a time would make personal visits.
3. We scripted our message and role-played together before going forth.
4. We crafted a list of requests to present to each seller. Requests were designed to urge a focus on safety first as well as lawful responsibility.
5. We share our experiences as things develop in hopes of improving our approach and possibility of successful engagement.

Sample Letter or Phone Call

Dear local business manager/owner,

Hello, my name is ___ from Goffstown. I/we represent a group from local churches who wish to engage in a thoughtful dialog with businesses so we can better understand the process you go through in selling guns and ammunition in our area. We do so out of respect for the Second Amendment of the U.S. Constitution and with concern for the safety of gun owners and fellow citizens of our neighborhoods.

We would like to sit down with you (or come in at a time convenient for you) to find out how you handle gun sales.

We hope we will find that gun sales in your shop follow the recommendations below. If that is so, we will happily let people know that you are actively supporting a responsible and safe approach to gun ownership.

Thank You,
PeaceMeals Goffstown
(contact information)

Recommendations for Gun Sales

Out of respect for the Second Amendment of the U.S. Constitution and with concern for the safety of gun owners and fellow citizens of our neighborhoods, I follow these guidelines for the sale of firearms in my place of business:

1. Require and keep on file for six months a photo, videotape, or digital image ID of each buyer.
2. Run NICS (National Instant Criminal Background Check System) background checks on each buyer and don't hand over

the firearm until such check is completed. (92 percent of NICS checks are completed immediately on the phone. Others within three days.)

3. In compliance with Federal Law my shop does not sell to any of the following:
    *   Minor
    *   Dishonorably discharged from military
    *   Federal felon
    *   Unlawfully in the U.S.
    *   Suspected of using a controlled substance or under the influence of alcohol or drugs
    *   Mentally ill
    *   Fugitive from justice
    *   Imprisoned for crime resulting in more than one year incarceration
4. If I have doubts about the stability of a customer I say no to the sale or ask them to wait a few days.

I do my best to uphold these reasonable recommendations for the responsible selling of guns in my community.

Questions We Might Ask Include

1. How do you deal with people you aren't so sure about?
2. What would I need to show you or what would you ask of me before selling me a firearm?

The Reverend Bill Exner is the rector of St. Matthew's Episcopal Church, Goffstown, New Hampshire. He can be reached at exner@comcast.net.

Note: The Peace Meal Project is also the name of a ministry in many Episcopal churches that can be found throughout the United States. For many of them, these began as a free fellowship meal for all, served weekly or monthly in a parish hall, with an offering of Evening Prayer at the conclusion of the meal. Calling this meal program the Peace Meal Project stems from knowing that a meal is only a small piece of the puzzle when it comes to addressing poverty, inequality, and loneliness. Sharing a fellowship meal together brings the community closer to the reign of God that all hope for—a community of justice, peace, and dignity for all people.

For Reflection

1. Where is your story in this story?
2. Where do you see God?
3. What causes you to pause and rethink your previous assumptions?
4. What cries out to you?
5. What calls to you?

Go Deeper

1. What would it take to form an Episcopal Peace Fellowship chapter in your congregation?
2. How might you (or your congregation) develop a relationship with gun shop owners in your town or city?
3. Are there other churches in your area that might partner with you for such advocacy work, whether it is contacting local gun dealers, offering a free meal in your parish on a regular basis, or inviting the homeless to join you for a meal or evening worship?

Inspiring Mission

Wendy Johnson, Beth Crow, and Cookie Cantwell

> *The Spirit of the Lord is upon me, because he has anointed me to bring good news to the poor. He has sent me to proclaim release to the captives and recovery of sight to the blind, to let the oppressed go free, to proclaim the year of the Lord's favor.* (Luke 4:18–19)

Mission is at the very heart of who we are as Christians. It is through mission that we understand the way in which God calls each one of us individually and communally to live and act in this world. Mission experiences, cultural immersion opportunities, and pilgrimages are integral components of Christian faith formation. They are opportunities for participants to go deeper into their faith journey, explore their innermost thoughts and beliefs, and develop a new understanding of our interconnectedness as the basis for peace.

Attitudes and practices related to mission and service have changed considerably in recent years, shifting away from "doing to" or "doing for" toward "doing with" or "being with." The core values and operational principles underlying the work of Inspiring Mission reflect these shifts.

Be forewarned: "doing with" and "being with" call for a bigger personal commitment than simply doing a job for someone or visiting a religious shrine. But they also lead to richer, more rewarding experiences. To achieve that end, we believe that transformational Episcopal mission experiences must embrace these five core values:

Episcopal

Mission being undertaken by Episcopal communities should be deeply embedded in the Episcopal tradition, incorporating our unique understanding of community, prayer, ritual, and liturgy into every aspect of the journey. From beginning the day with prayer to ending the day in reflection and conversation, these journeys should be executed in a way that leads participants to understand how their faith tradition both informs and enhances their lives. As you depart for a mission experience or pilgrimage, reflect on the ways your community embraces the Episcopal tradition and incorporate them into your journey. Be sure to pack your Book of Common Prayer, Bible, and other prayer/inspiration resources. Organize a cycle of daily prayer and, if possible, a Eucharist into the experience. Finally, watch for ways in which you can connect a deep understanding of being an Episcopalian with the experiences you are having on your journey.

Respectful

Mission experiences must respect the dignity and integrity of every community and individual by being open to diverse cultural expressions. This will require participants to lay aside their assumptions in an effort to understand the other community's cultural and interpersonal norms. This requires research and preparation into the culture of the community you are visiting, and a willingness to examine your own cultural assumptions. Participants should spend significant time preparing spiritually and emotionally for the journey and, while traveling, set aside time for reflection and/or journaling each day.

Mutual

All too often, participants in a mission experience volunteer to "help" another community or organization. This leads to the creation of an "us" and "them" or "haves" and "have-nots" understanding of our world. It is the essence of being in "service to." However, transformational mission experiences embrace the idea that participants are "serving with" each other—whether they are from the community being visited or the traveling community. This is accomplished through open and respectful dialogue before the work commences and in a deep understanding of the mutuality of the experience while you are in community.

Sustainable

Each mission experience or pilgrimage should be designed in a way that fosters long-term growth and sustainability. As much as possible, participating communities should openly discuss project possibilities and work opportunities that embrace each community's gifts and needs. This can require gifts and needs assessment work on the part of both communities and a commitment to ongoing conversation as the exact nature of the commitment evolves as the planning proceeds.

During pilgrimages, participants can reflect on the ways in which their viewpoints and values are challenged and expanded during the experience—and how that will have a long-term and sustainable impact on how they will choose to live in peace when they return from the journey.

Holistic

Mission experiences and pilgrimages should be intentionally designed to address the multiple needs and desires of the individuals and communities participating. This includes the emotional, physical, spiritual, cultural, and practical elements of each individual and community. While it can seem like a lot to undertake, it is important for leaders to thoroughly consider each of these elements and address them appropriately.

- What is the capacity for physical labor of each participant?
- Where is each participant spiritually? Do you share a common understanding of Christianity and worship? Is everyone an Episcopalian? If not, how can you broaden your spiritual exercises to incorporate those new to the tradition?
- Are there cultural norms that need to be embraced? Does anyone have worship or personal needs that should be accommodated?
- What are the emotional needs of participants? Is anyone experiencing something notable in their personal lives that may impact the experience?

Wendy Johnson (Diocese of Minneapolis), **Beth Crow** (Diocese of North Carolina), and **Cookie Cantwell** (Diocese of East Carolina) are collaborators in *Inspiring Mission* (www.inspiringmission.com), an organization dedicated to facilitating mission experiences, pilgrimages, and providing education on mission in the Episcopal Church. They have a combined seventy-five years of experience in youth ministry, leading domestic and international mission experiences and pilgrimages. They are coauthors of the *Episcopal Youth in Mission Manual* (www.episcopalchurch.org/page/episcopal-youth-mission-manual), which explores each of the concepts described here in more depth. They work in partnership with Bronwyn Clark Skov, team leader, Formation and Congregational Development and Officer, Youth Ministries.

For Reflection

1. Where is your story in this story?
2. Where do you see God?
3. What causes you to pause and rethink your previous assumptions?
4. What cries out to you?
5. What calls to you?

Go Deeper

1. How can we grow deeper in our unique Episcopal understanding of Christianity by undertaking mission experiences and pilgrimages?
2. How is peace established when we lay aside our inclination to judge other individuals and communities by our own norms and standards and look for the beauty in the ways we all represent our cultural contexts?
3. How can we create peace when we meet each other as equal participants rather than as people to be helped?
4. Is it possible to build a relationship with another individual or community without at the same time fostering peace?
5. How is our understanding of "difference" impacted when we see each other as multifaceted individuals and communities rather than stereotypes?

PRAY:
THE WORK

"Faith, Hope, Love" Acrylic on canvas ©2014 Roger Hutchison.
Used with permission.

Prayers and Litanies

A Litany of Peace[66] *Psalm 37 Noli aemulari*

Do not fear because of the wicked; do not be envious of the wrongdoers

For they will soon fade like the grass, and wither like the green herb.

Trust in the LORD, and do what is good, so that you will live in the land and enjoy security.

Take delight in the LORD, and God will give you the desires of your heart.

Be still before the LORD, and wait patiently for God;

Do not fear over those who prosper in their way, over those who carry out evil devices.

Refrain from anger and forsake wrath.

Do not fear: it leads only to evil.

The wicked plot against the righteous, gnash their teeth at them;

66   From the closing Eucharist at "Reclaiming the Gospel of Peace," April 11, 2014

But, the Lord laughs at the wicked and sees that their day is coming.

The wicked draw their sword and bend their bows to bring down the poor and needy, to kill those who walk uprightly;

Their sword shall enter their own heart, and their bows shall be broken.

Better is a little that the righteous person has

Than the abundance of many wicked.

The wicked borrow and do not pay back

But the righteous are generous and keep giving.

Our steps are made firm by the LORD when God delights in our way.

Though we stumble, we shall not fall headlong, for the Lord holds us by the hand.

Depart from evil, and do what is good; so you may abide forever.

The LORD loves justice and will not forsake the faithful.

The wicked watch for the righteous, and seek to kill them.

The LORD will not abandon them to their power, or let them be condemned when they are brought to trial.

The salvation of the righteous is from the LORD

God is their refuge in the time of trouble.

The Lord helps them and rescues them

God rescues them from the wicked, and saves them because they take refuge in the LORD.

The Prayers of the People[67]

May we call upon God to inspire us to do the work of being peacemakers.

Eternal God, in whom the whole family of earth is one, breathe your spirit into our hearts that we may establish a global community of trust and fellowship, justice and peace.

Illumine the darkness of our minds that we may see your light, think your thoughts, and serve your glory by advancing the greater good of all people.

Silence

Reform, O God, the passions and designs of our hearts.

Let your steady hand guide the nations, and bring forth out of our discord a harmony more perfect than we can conceive—a new humility, a new understanding, a new purity and sincerity, a new sense of truth, and a new hunger and thirst for your love to rule the earth.

Silence

Grant, O God, that all leaders may approach every question of foreign and domestic policy from your point of view, that their noblest thoughts may be purified and strengthened.

Help us check in ourselves and in others every temper which makes for violence, and all promptings of self-assertion, isolation, and arrogance, that we may understand the aspirations of other countries, and other peoples, and may gladly do what lies in us to remove every misunderstanding, thus serving the welfare of all people.

Silence

O God, in whom is the power of perfect understanding: heal the dissensions which divide us.

Bring us back into that unity of love, which is the likeness of your nature.

---

67   From the Closing Eucharist at "Reclaiming the Gospel of Peace," April 22, 2014

Silence

Holy God, you have made of one blood all nations that dwell upon earth. Look with mercy upon us, and drive away our evil passions of fear and hatred.

Grant that united in good will we may live together in charity and joy, each in the praise of great achievements, in rivalry of good and beneficent deeds, and sharing in truthful and just dealings with one another.

Silence

Increase, O God, the spirit of neighborliness among all who dwell on earth, that in peril we may uphold one another, in suffering tend one another, and in loneliness befriend one another.

Grant us brave and enduring hearts that we may be strengthened, until the strife of these days be ended and you give peace in our time; through Jesus Christ our Lord. Amen.

A Litany on the Pebbles of Love[68]

Prior to this litany, distribute a small stone to each participant, or have a bowl of small pebbles in the center or front of those gathered to pray.

In the face of the boulders of disrespect for all who are different,

Let us be pebbles of respect for the dignity and diversity of every person.

In the face of the boulders of having it always my way,

Let us be pebbles of mutuality.

In the face of the boulders of tuning out others,

Let us be pebbles of listening.

In the face of the boulders of grudges and retaliation,

Let us be pebbles of forgiving love.

In the face of the boulders of using more than our share,

Let us be pebbles of simple sufficiency.

In the face of the boulders of violence against other species and the earth herself,

---

68   From the Institute of Peace and Justice, http://www.ipj-ppj.org.

Let us be pebbles of beauty and respect.

In the face of the boulders of violent entertainment,

Let us be pebbles of playfulness.

In the face of the boulders of discrimination and exploitation because of race, age, gender, or sexual orientation,

Let us be pebbles solidarity.

In the face of escalating violence, escalate love as participants take their pebbles and pray the prayer attributed to St. Francis.

Litany on the Nonviolence of Jesus[69]

If you, even you, had only recognized on this day the things that make for peace! (Luke 19:42)

Jesus, you wept over Jerusalem and its disregard of Samaritans and lepers, and you weep today over the escalating violence of racism and hate in our own society and world.
    Jesus, in the face of escalating violence,

Let us escalate love.
Jesus, you wept over Jerusalem and its humiliating occupation by the Roman Empire, and you weep today over the escalating violence of terrorism and humiliating occupation in your Holy Land.
    Jesus, in the face of escalating violence,

Let us escalate love.
Jesus, you wept over Jerusalem and its exploitation of the poor, and you weep today over the escalating violence of poverty in our own society and world.
    Jesus, in the face of escalating violence,

Let us escalate love.
Jesus, you wept over Jerusalem and its disregard of women and children, and you weep today over escalating violence against women and children in our own society and world.
    Jesus, in the face of escalating violence,

---

69   From the Institute of Peace and Justice, www.ipj-ppj.org.

Let us escalate love.

Jesus, you wept over Jerusalem and its deadly use of weapons of violence, and you weep today over the proliferation of the weapons of violence, from handguns to nuclear bombs, in our own society and world.

Jesus, in the face of escalating violence,

Let us escalate love.

Jesus, you wept over Jerusalem where capital punishment was rampant, and you weep today over the escalating use of capital punishment in our own society.

Jesus, in the face of escalating violence,

Let us escalate love.

Jesus, you wept over Jerusalem where the forces of domination were everywhere, and you weep today over the escalating domination—all the 'isms—in our own society and world.

Jesus, in the face of escalating violence,

Let us escalate love.

Prayers

O God, you made us in your own image and redeemed us through Jesus your Son: Look with compassion on the whole human family; take away the arrogance and hatred which infect our hearts; break down the walls that separate us; unite us in bonds of love; and work through our struggle and confusion to accomplish your purposes on earth; that, in your good time, all nations and races may serve you in harmony around your heavenly throne; through Jesus Christ our Lord. Amen. (*For the Human Family*, Book of Common Prayer, 815)

Almighty God, kindle, we pray, in every heart the true love of peace, and guide with your wisdom those who take counsel for the nations of the earth, that in tranquility your dominion may increase until the earth is filled with the knowledge of your love; through Jesus Christ our Lord, who lives and reigns with you, in the unity of the Holy Spirit, one God, now and for ever. Amen. (*Collect for Peace*, Book of Common Prayer, 258)

O God, you have bound us together in a common life. Help us, in the midst of our struggles for justice and truth, to confront one another without hatred or bitterness, and to work together with mutual forbearance and respect; through Jesus Christ our Lord. Amen. (*In Times of Conflict*, Book of Common Prayer, 824)

Lord, make us instruments of your peace. Where there is hatred, let us sow love; where there is injury, pardon; where there is discord, union; where there is doubt, faith; where there is despair, hope; where there is darkness, light; where there is sadness, joy. Grant that we may not so much seek to be consoled as to console; to be understood as to understand; to be loved as to love. For it is in giving that we receive; it is in pardoning that we are pardoned; and it is in dying that we are born to eternal life. Amen. (*A Prayer attributed to St. Francis of Assisi*, Book of Common Prayer, 833)

Almighty God, you proclaim your truth in every age by many voices: Direct, in our time, we pray, those who speak where many listen and write what many read; that they may do their part in making the heart of this people wise, its mind sound, and its will righteous; to the honor of Jesus Christ our Lord. Amen. (*For those who Influence Public Opinion*, Book of Common Prayer, 827)

God of justice and mercy, we cry out to you from a land dominated by gun violence. Empower the members of Congress with such wisdom, insight, and courage that they will pass effective legislation against the murders and injuries that now rage as an epidemic among us. Help all of us to step forward to release our nation from bondage to weapons and enslavement to fear. May we greet with joy the new freedom you intend for this land. All this we ask in the name of Jesus our liberator, the prince of peace. Amen. (*Prayer for Gun Violence Prevention* by The Reverend Charles Hoffacker, Parish of St. Monica and St. James, Capitol Hill, Washington, DC.)

The Way of the Cross

The Way of the Cross: Challenging a Culture of Violence was held on March 25, 2013, in Washington, DC. The booklet of prayers and reflections, compiled by the Episcopal Church in Connecticut, can be downloaded, along with other resources at https://www.episcopalct. org/Beliefs-and-Practices/Challenging-Violence/

Anointed for Peace: A Service of Healing and Hope

Stephen C. Holton

This liturgy was offered on Memorial Day in 2014, the 100ᵗʰ anniversary of World War I.

Invocation
Leader: Holy, holy, holy, is the Lord God of Hosts.
People: The whole earth is full of his Glory.

Prayers for Those Who Have Died

The Word of God *Genesis 4:3–16*
Cain said to his brother Abel, "Let us go out into the field." And when they were in the field, Cain rose up against his brother Abel, and killed him. Then the Lord said to Cain, "Where is your brother Abel?" He said, "I do not know; am I my brother's keeper?" And the Lord said, "What have you done? Listen; your brother's blood is crying out to me from the ground! And now you are cursed from the ground, which has opened its mouth to receive your brother's blood from your hand. When you till the ground, it will no longer yield to you its strength; you will be a fugitive and a wanderer on the earth." Cain said to the Lord, "My punishment is greater than I can bear! Today you have driven me away from the soil, and

I shall be hidden from your face; I shall be a fugitive and a wanderer on the earth, and anyone who meets me may kill me." Then the Lord said to him, "Not so! Whoever kills Cain will suffer a seven fold vengeance." And the Lord put a mark on Cain so that no one who came upon him would kill him (vv. 8–15).

Conversation *Precious Lord, take my hand*
God did not react to Cain's violence. Scripture says, six times, that Cain has killed his brother. It does not ignore the violence. Neither should we. The seventh time, God sends Cain away. The seventh time, God rests from anger, and reasserts life and love. We can do the same.

Sit with someone you do not know. One at a time, each speak to the other for five minutes of the violence he/she has done or allowed in thought, word, or deed. Then speak for five minutes each; forgiving violence you have endured. Yet even Jesus did not forgive directly. He asked God to "forgive them . . . for they know not what they do."

Psalm 51

Prayers of Concern about Violence and for Peace

Anointing of Hands

Clench your fists to hold the violence one last time. Then drop it. Put down the burden of violence, and take up the Gospel of Peace

Hymn *O Lord, hear my prayer (Taizé Community)*

The Peace *Greet everyone with the words: "Peace be with you."*

The World Peace Prayer

Lead me from death to life
From falsehood to truth;
Lead me from despair to hope,
From fear to trust;
Lead me from hate to love,
From war to peace,
Let peace fill our heart, our world, our universe.

Hymn 719 *Oh beautiful, for spacious skies*

The Reverend Stephen C. Holton is the assistant for Christian formation at St. Barnabas Episcopal Church in Irvington, New York.

With a Mission Enterprise Zone grant from the Episcopal Church, he developed Warriors of the Dream, a youth program in Harlem that gathers youth of many faiths with artists, community leaders, and elders to nurture gifts, teach dialogue skills, develop leaders, and build the neighborhood.

ENGAGE:
THE NEXT STEPS

Hartford, Connecticut was selected as the kick-off site for "Raise the Caliber," a national advocacy campaign to end illegal gun violence. Central to the campaign was the unveiling of a public art installation by Michael Kalish. The work, a 30-foot high sculpture created from 2,000 lbs. of illegal guns bought off the streets through voluntary gun buybacks, was unveiled in September 2014 and will travel to cities across the country in 2015. Photo ©2014 Marc Yves Regis. Used with permission.

Action Guide

There are a variety of avenues that can be taken to reflect upon this book in a group setting. In a faith community, it can be a focal point for an Advent or Lenten evening adult program that is bracketed by a meal and worship. It can be a study series offered during a Sunday morning education time.

However, reflection tends to be an inward process. That is important, but being a disciple of Jesus Christ means to put one's faith into action. Hopefully the essays within this book have stirred up within you the desire to do something more, to put these words into action, to be silent no longer. Whether it is individually or as part of your faith community, explore the issues that are raised within these pages on a deeper level—violence, mental health, poverty, racism, gun laws, education—and develop ways to address them through local, national, or even global means.

The preliminary work you do as a group will be most important before attempting to implement any action. Pray together. Build community and share stories with one another before addressing the next steps. Pray some more. Caitlin Cecella offers a beginning point in chapter 1 that she learned from Bishop Eugene Sutton (adapted):

1. Stand up
2. Say your name and where you live
3. Share why you have come to this gathering

This book can be discussed chapter-by-chapter or focused on a specific issue related to gun violence, such as legislation, advocacy, or mental health. Your group may wish to have a chance to express which issue they feel is most pressing or one that the whole group can get behind for further action steps. It provides rich material for conversation and a challenge for engagement. Tap into the prayers, Scripture, reflection questions, and examples that have been given here. Seek out what is occurring in your local community as well as on the state level. But build community with one another first. Before beginning any gathering, follow Eric Law's process of "Mutual Invitation" (below) and "Rights, Respect, and Responsibilities" (Chapter 28) for setting up group norms.

It is hoped that groups who come together to consider this book will not experience it as a short-term study, but one that becomes a lifelong normative commitment toward working for a more peaceful, hopeful, and just society.

Guidelines for Small Group Discussion

Reclaiming the Gospel of Peace explores deep-rooted social and spiritual issues such as mental health, constitutional rights, race, poverty, class, and violence. Creating a safe space for such conversations is essential in order for individuals to be fully engaged and participate at a level that promotes growth and action.

Eric Law also offers an easy-to-follow model of establishing group norms beginning any meeting, through his "Respectful Communication Guidelines":[70]

> **R** = Take RESPONSIBILITY for what you say and feel with blaming others
> **E** = EMPATHETIC listening
> **S** = Be SENSTIVE to differences in communication styles

---

70   Law, Erik H. F. *The Bush Was Blazing But Not Consumed* (St. Louis, MO: Chalice Press, 1996), 87.

P = PONDER what your hear and feel before you speak.

E = EXAMINE your own assumptions and perceptions

C = Keep CONFIDENTIALITY

T = TOLERATE ambiguity because we are *not* here to debate who is right or wrong.

There are several specific models for creating an environment for open discussion. Parker Palmer's "circles of trust" as explored in *A Hidden Wholeness: The Journey Toward an Undivided Life* (San Francisco: Jossey-Bass, 1994) is "a space between us that honors the soul." He shows how people in settings ranging from friendship to organizational life can support each other on the journey toward living "divided no more."

Eric H. F. Law has a wonderful technique for active listening in his work, *The Wolf Shall Dwell With the Lamb* (St. Louis, MO: Chalice Press, 1993). The technique is presented as a tool for multicultural conversation and dialogue, but it seems valuable for any number of settings and circumstances. Below is an adaptation of Law's "Mutual Invitation" technique.

1. Begin by letting everyone know the amount of time provided for the group's conversation.
2. Carefully name the topic to be discussed, the information to be shared, or the question(s) to be answered.
3. Read the following directions: In order to ensure that everyone who wants to share has the opportunity to speak, we will proceed in the following way. The leader/convener will share first. After that person has spoken, he or she invites another person to share. The person whom you invite does not need to be the person next to you. After the next person has spoken, that person is given the privilege to invite another person to share. If the person invited does not wish to say anything, that person simply says, "pass" and proceeds to invite another to share. This process is followed until everyone has been invited to speak.
4. The process is a discipline for the group that allows everyone to share the power of selection and everyone to share the power of response. Be patient with one another. Allow time between invitations to hear what has been said. Silence is welcome. A person may wish to pass on speaking, but no one should be allowed to pass on inviting. No one should invite for another. If the person who is supposed to invite forgets to do so, remind them that they have the privilege of selection.

Chapter Reflection Questions

At the conclusion of each chapter, a series of questions is asked for reflection. All of them begin with these five questions as a starting point for personal thoughts or group discussion. They are followed by specific questions to the chapter.

1. Where is your story in this story?
2. Where do you see God?
3. What causes you to pause and rethink your previous assumptions?
4. What cries out to you?
5. What calls to you?

Topical Study

Instead of gathering to discuss *Reclaiming the Gospel of Peace* chapter by chapter, you may wish to focus on the topics or themes that run throughout the text. Any of the questions or Scripture can be used or modified to fit the topics, of which a few are listed here:

- The Second Amendment
- Violence (gun, partner-to-partner)
- Elder abuse
- Child abuse
- Domestic violence
- Poverty
- Racism
- War
- Education
- Justice
- Activism and organizing
- The Baptismal Covenant
- Gun laws
- Reconciliation

Guidelines for Bible Study (optional)

Scripture is an important element to any group gathering or action step. It should ground all conversations and decision-making. Many pieces of Scripture are used throughout this book and can be used for reflection. One method is the Indaba (African) Bible Study, which offers a means for personal reflection and group insights that may be helpful as the group prepares to discuss each chapter or theme.

1. One person reads the Scripture passage slowly.
2. Each person identifies the word or phrase that catches his or her attention (1 minute).
3. Each shares the word or phrase around the group (3–5 minutes, no discussion).
4. Another person reads the passage slowly (from a different translation, if possible).
5. Each person identifies where this passage touches his or her life today (1 minute).
6. Each shares (3–5 minutes, no discussion).
7. Passage is read a third time (another reader and translation, if possible).
8. Each person names or writes, "From what I've heard and shared, what do I believe God wants me to do or be? Is God inviting me to change in any way?" (5 minutes).
9. Each person shares his or her answer (5–10 minutes, no discussion).
10. Each prays for the person on their right, naming what was shared in the other steps (5 minutes).
11. Close with the Lord's Prayer and silence.

The following Scriptures may be especially appropriate

Psalm 34	Habbakuk 1:1–17	Luke 6:20–26
Psalm 72:1–4	Matthew 5:3–12	Acts 4:24–30
Isaiah 2:3–5	Matthew 5:43–48	1 Corinthians 4:16–21
Micah 4:1–5	Matthew 26:52	Ephesians 2:13–18

Possible Action Steps

1. Lobby your state and national representatives on issues such as:
   - *Background checks:* Establish a universal background check system for all persons purchasing a firearm from any seller.
   - *High-risk individuals:* Expand the set of conditions that disqualify an individual from legally purchasing a firearm.
   - *Mental health:* Focus federal restrictions on gun purchases by persons with serious mental illness or the dangerousness of the individual.

- *Trafficking and dealer licensing:* Appoint a permanent director to ATF and provide the agency with the authority to develop a range of sanctions for gun dealers who violate gun sales or other laws.
- *Personalized guns:* Provide financial incentives to states to mandate childproof or personalized guns.
- *Assault weapons and high-capacity magazines*: Ban the future sale of assault weapons and the future sale and possession of large-capacity ammunition magazines.
- *Research funds:* Provide adequate federal funds to the Centers for Disease Control and Prevention, National Institutes of Health, and National Institute of Justice for research into the causes and solutions of gun violence.

2. Meet with other faith traditions in your community to collaborate and join efforts to be a witness to nonviolence in your city or town.
3. Hold an adult forum series, inviting community organizers and leaders to speak on issues of violence, mental health, bullying, partner-to-partner abuse, poverty, and/or racism.
4. Join the Episcopal Public Policy Network and your diocesan chapter to see how you can get involved.

28

Rights, Respect, and Responsibilities[71]

Eric H. F. Law

A process to help community members arrive at a set of community principles that they can affirm and uphold to enhance community life.

How to Use This Process

The following is a set of worksheets that participants will complete in a one- to two-hour period. The instructions are on the worksheets themselves. The facilitator needs only to guide the participants through the process.

RIGHTS

Webster's dictionary defines right *as "that which a person has a just claim to; power, privilege, etc. that belongs to a person by law, nature, or traditions."*

1. What are your rights as a member of this community? (Reflect on this on your own and write your ideas below.)

71 Erik H. F. Law, *Inclusion: Making Room for Grace* (St. Louis, MO: Chalice Press, 2000), 120–24. Used with permission.

2. Move around the room and collect at least two different responses to question 1 from other participants and write them below:
3. Review your answers to questions 1 and 2. What are some concerns that you have regarding your rights and others' rights? (For example, potential conflicts, misinterpretation, dealing with controversy, etc.)

RESPECT

1. Complete the following sentence:
    I know I am respected when . . .

2. Move around the room and collect from others two responses that differ from yours.
    a. I know I am respected when . . .

    b. I know I am respected when . . .

3. Compare the three responses and reflect on the following:
    What are the reasons behind the different perceptions of respect?

RESPONSIBLITIES

1. What are your responsibilities in upholding your own rights in this community?

    One of your responsibilities to uphold your own rights is to communicate with others who you are and how you would like to be treated.
    a. What do others need to know about you for you to feel included?

In what ways can you communicate this information to others in the community?

    b. What kind of support do you need to effectively communicate who you are and how you would like to be treated as a member of this community? (Support can come in the form of policy, support group, regular dialogue session, one-on-one sharing, etc.)

2. What are your responsibilities in upholding others' rights in this community?

    a. Review your learning from the discussions on rights and respect.
        What concrete behavior and attitude adjustments will you make in order to better respect others' rights?

    b. If you observed that someone's rights were not respected in this community, what would you do?

3. What are your responsibilities in enabling others in your community to better respect one another's rights?

Possible Community Covenant

1. Review the learning from this activity so far.
2. List three things that you would do to fulfill your responsibilities in respecting and upholding the rights of each person in this community.
    a.

b.

c.

3. List three things that you would NOT do to fulfill your responsibilities to respect and uphold the rights of each person in this
   community.
   a.

   b.

   c.

4. Submit your list to a central person in your community, who
   will collect and collage the information. The community will
   meet again to read and digest the complete list and arrive at a
   community covenant that everyone can agree to uphold.

———

The Reverend Erik H. F. Law, an Episcopal priest, is the founder
and executive director of the Kaleidoscope Institute, the mission of
which is to create inclusive and sustainable churches and communities. For more than twenty years, he has provided transformative
and comprehensive training and resources for churches and ministries in all major church denominations in the United States. He
blogs at *The Sustainist: Spirituality for Sustainable Communities in a
Networked World.* http://ehflaw.typepad.com/blog/

29

Annotated Bibliography and Resource List

Books to Assist Your Individual or Group Learning

Ackerman, Peter, and Jack DuVall. *A Force More Powerful: A Century of Non-Violent Conflict* (New York: Palgrave MacMillan, 2000) shows how popular movements used nonviolent action to overthrow dictators, obstruct military invaders, and secure human rights in country after country, over the past century. The authors depict how nonviolent sanctions—such as protests, strikes, and boycotts—separate brutal regimes from their means of control. They tell inside stories—how Danes outmaneuvered the Nazis, Solidarity defeated Polish communism, and mass action removed a Chilean dictator—and also how nonviolent power is changing the world today, from Burma to Serbia. PBS also did a documentary based on the book. www.aforcemorepowerful.org

Battle, Michael. *Ubuntu: I in You and You in Me* (New York: Seabury, 2009). Ubuntu is an African way of seeing the world—and the people in it—as an intricate web of relationships. Practicing Ubuntu means entering deeply into the compassionate, forgiving love of the Gospel, encouraging harmony and interdependence among individuals and communities.

Brueggemann, Walter. *Prayers for a Privileged People* (Nashville: Abingdon, 2008) offers prayers for proclaiming peace, justice, righteousness, and joy in a world that is far from the dream of God. A resource for worship and meetings.

Kraybill, Donald A. *Amish Grace: How Forgiveness Transcended Tragedy* (San Francisco: Jossey-Bass, 2010). Explores the many questions raised by the killing of five children in a one-room Amish schoolhouse in Nichol Mines, Pennsylvania, in 2006 by a gunman in which the grieving community attended the funeral of the killer immediately following the funerals where they had buried their own. The Amish act of forgiveness offers a witness of faith.

Larson, Erik. *Lethal Passage: The Story of a Gun* (New York: Random House, 2011) is the story of how a bullied boy takes out his anger using a gun at school. While based on an event in 1988, Larson's thorough research and story is still applicable today.

Law, Eric H. F. *Inclusion: Making Room for Grace* (St. Louis, MO: Chalice Press, 2000) offers practical and theological based approaches to enable a community to act inclusively when its boundary is challenged. Within this book Eric has developed a process and model to help a community extend its boundary to include an outsider's experience and perspective in a constructive and faithful way. His "Rights, Respect, and Responsibilities" offer a process for any group to develop a set of community principles before delving into conversations on topics that may be divisive.

Law, Eric H. F. *The Wolf Shall Dwell With the Lamb* (St. Louis, MO: Chalice Press, 1993) offers a technique, "Mutual Invitation," for multicultural conversation and dialogue, which is valuable for any number of settings and circumstances.

Palmer, Parker. *A Hidden Wholeness: The Journey Toward an Undivided Life* (San Francisco: Jossey-Bass, 1994). Using illustrations and practical experience he gained while living at Pendle Hill, a Quaker center for study and contemplation near Philadelphia, Palmer discusses the many ways in which "circles of trust" can support the quest for integrity and meaning as he outlines the key practices of these circles, including speaking center-to-center, deep listening, asking open and honest questions, and honoring silence.

Simpson, Amy. *Troubled Minds: Mental Illness and the Church's Mission* (Downer's Grove, IL: InterVarsity Press, 2013) provides a look at the social and physical realities of mental illness and explores new possibilities for ministry to this stigmatized group, calling the church to a renewed commitment to people who suffer from mental illness and their families that suffer with them.

Smiley, Tavis, and Cornel West. *The Rich and the Rest of Us: A Poverty Manifesto* (New York: SmileyBooks, 2012) was the focus of a diocesan-wide book discussion held in the Diocese of Massachusetts during Lent 2013. Bishop M. Thomas Shaw, SSJE, described the book as one that "asks us to re-examine some of our assumptions about poverty" and "a way to begin to educate ourselves about poverty, one of the root causes of violence." The book study came in response to the shooting death of nineteen-year-old Jorge Fuentes, a young leader in a youth program at St. Stephen's Episcopal Church, Boston. You can download the study guide here: http://www.diomass.org/webfm_send/1955.

Tutu, Desmond. *No Future Without Forgiveness* (Colorado Springs, CO: Image, 2000) offers his reflections on the profound wisdom he gained by helping South Africa through the painful experience of moving from apartheid and despotism to reconciliation.

Webster, Daniel W., and Jon S. Vernick, eds. *Reducing Gun Violence in America: Informing Policy with Evidence and Analysis* (Baltimore, MD: Johns Hopkins University Press, 2013) is the result of more than twenty of the world's leading experts on gun violence and policy convened by the Johns Hopkins University to summarize relevant research and recommend policies that are both constitutional and have broad public support. Collected for the first time in one volume, this reliable, empirical research and legal analysis will help lawmakers, opinion leaders, and concerned citizens identify policy changes to address mass shootings, along with the less-publicized gun violence that takes an average of eighty lives every day.

Winkler, Adam. *Gunfight: The Battle Over the Right to Bear Arms* (New York: W.W. Norton & Company, 2013) shares the history (and controversies) of gun use and ownership in the United States. The author shows that we can have both an individual right to have guns for self-defense and, at the same time, laws designed to improve gun safety. His thesis is that the right to bear arms and gun control are not mutually exclusive propositions and that race and racism is often at the heart of the issue.

Organizations to Support Your Action

Bishops United Against Gun Violence is a coalition of Episcopal bishops that urges our cities, states, and nation to adapt policies and pass legislation that will reduce the number of Americans killed and wounded by gunfire. http://bishopsagainstgunviolence.org

Creating a Culture of Peace (CCP) is a nationwide program for community-based peacemaking. The innovative design of CCP provides a holistic and practical foundation in spiritually grounded active nonviolence. Participants come to recognize their own power for making personal and social changes without violence and improve their skills for respectful engagement with opponents, instead of confrontation that polarizes and demonizes. CCP training is an incubator for participants to raise issues that most concern them, such as group controversy and conflict, neighborhood violence, domestic violence, climate change, war and militarism, discrimination, video games, homelessness, peace education, and health care. www.creatingacultureofpeace.org

The Episcopal Peace Fellowship (EPF) is a national organization connecting all who seek a deliberate response to injustice and violence and want to pray, study, and take action for justice and peace in our communities, our church, and the world. We are called to do justice, dismantle violence, and strive to be peacemakers. EPF chapters are regionally based and work on local peace initiatives within their parish and communities as well as on national and international issues. They sponsor and cosponsor prayer and public witness such as peace vigils, liturgies, service projects, and demonstrations. http://epfnational.org

Episcopal Public Policy Network (EPPN) is a grassroots network of Episcopalians across the country dedicated to carrying out the Baptismal Covenant call to "strive for justice and peace" through the active ministry of public policy advocacy. The EPPN is a part of The Episcopal Church Office of Government Relations located in Washington, DC. The actions, programs, and ministry of the Office of Government Relations are based entirely on policies approved by the church meeting in General Convention or by the Executive Council. The online EPPN action center is a tool kit for your faithful activism and community involvement, including information about your congressional representatives, templates for writing to them, and other information. http://advocacy.episcopalchurch.org/home

FaithTrust Institute is a national multifaith training and education organization that is working to end sexual and domestic violence. FaithTrust Institute provides faith communities and advocates with the tools and knowledge they need to address the faith and cultural issues related to abuse. www.cpsdv.org

Faiths United to Prevent Gun Violence, a diverse coalition of denominations and faith-based organizations united by the call of their faiths to confront America's gun violence epidemic and to rally support for policies that reduce death and injury from gunfire, was formed on Martin Luther King Day, January 17, 2011. http://faithsagainstgunviolence.org

Institute for Peace and Justice is an independent, interfaith, not-for-profit organization in St. Louis that has focused on issues of peace and justice since 1970. With the development of **Families Against Violence Advocacy Network** (FAVAN) IPJ's advocacy priorities expanded to include gun violence, violence in the media, violence in schools, domestic violence, and children's voices. They have developed numerous curricula and programs for public schools and religious education programs. In addition to the Pledge of Nonviolence developed for families, schools, and churches, they publish a lectionary-based worship bulletin for children called "Peace Papers" that connect the Sunday readings to issues of peace and justice. www.ipj-ppj.org

Mayors Against Illegal Guns. In 2006, former New York City Mayor Michael Bloomberg and former Boston Mayor Thomas Menino founded Mayors Against Illegal Guns as a coalition of fifteen mayors. Since then, they have built a bipartisan group of more than one thousand current and former mayors from nearly every state to fight for commonsense gun laws. http://everytown.org/mayors/

Moms Demand Action. After the tragic shooting in Newtown, Connecticut, stay-at-home mom Shannon Watts decided to do something about it and channel what moms were feeling into a movement to stop everyday violence. What started as a single Facebook page has grown into a nationwide movement. In the past year, moms have taken on Starbucks for allowing customers to carry concealed, loaded guns in its stores—and won. They called on Facebook to crack down on illegal gun sales on its platform—and won. And they're calling on state and national lawmakers to enact commonsense gun laws that will protect our kids. http://everytown.org/moms/

National Episcopal Health Ministries (EHM) promotes health ministry in Episcopal congregations, assisting them to reclaim the gospel imperative of health and wholeness. Health ministry in a local congregation is an intentional ministry focusing on both healing and health, combining the ancient traditions of the Christian community and the knowledge and tools of modern health care. Part of their commitment is to reconciliation in a broken and fragmented world, and to that end, their resource has numerous links related to health care issues, violence, and gun violence. www.episcopalhealthministries.org

StopBullying.gov provides information from various government agencies on what bullying is, what cyber-bullying is, who is at risk, and how you can prevent and respond to bullying. www. stopbullying.gov

Gun Violence Resources

The Brady Campaign and the **Brady Center to Prevent Gun Violence** have a long and rich history of inspired and strong leadership on gun violence prevention, championing the reduction of gun death and injury in America for forty years. In November 1993, the organization scored a major federal legislative victory with the passage and signing of the Brady Law that requires background checks on all gun sales made at federally licensed firearm dealers. www. bradycampaign.org

The Campaign to Stop Gun Violence is a coalition of national organizations that are willing to take a stand to let policymakers know that we can and *must* stop the flow of illegal guns into our communities. Campaign members join by signing a general Statement of Principles encompassing a variety of gun policy positions that the majority of Americans embrace. Campaign efforts and programs include: a) Fostering research and education about gun violence; b) Supporting grassroots efforts to prevent gun violence; c) Advocating for commonsense gun policies like universal background checks and enhanced screening and training for individuals who carry guns in public. http://campaigntostopgunviolence.org

Gun Violence in America Study Materials from Washington National Cathedral offers numerous short (2–3 minutes) video clips on topics that are key to the gun violence prevention debate and challenge. The clips are excerpts from the full panel discussions, which may also be viewed in their complete state on DVD that are available for purchase for use in small groups, churches, and community gatherings. Other documents include the Gun Sabbath Weekend Program and a variety of sermons and statements regarding gun violence. www.nationalcathedral.org/gunviolence

Gun Violence Prevention: Congregational Toolkit from the Presbyterian Peace Fellowship offers a Bible study, conversation starters, worship resources, and other materials for congregations who wish to "Heed God's Call" for public witness. http://www. presbypeacefellowship.org/files/gunviolence/GVP%20Toolkit2.pdf

Gun Violence Prevention Curriculum from the Episcopal Peace Fellowship is a twenty-six-page booklet that serves as one way to raise awareness of gun violence as a spiritual and moral crisis and actively work toward achieving the peaceable kingdom. Five lesson plans (Guns in the U.S. Today, Gun Violence 101, Illegal Sales, Suicide, Supporting Those Who Grieve) for adult study are included, as well as worship materials. http://epfnational/what-about-guns

The Gun Violence Prevention Sabbath Weekend brings together people of faith—clergy, public leaders, advocates, victims, mothers and fathers, brothers and sisters—to explore how our faith inspires action toward commonsense solutions to help end the gun violence epidemic in America. A special project of Faiths United to Prevent Gun Violence and Washington National Cathedral, it began in 2013. Since then nearly one thousand places of worship in forty-six states and the District of Columbia have participated in the weekend that involves prayer, song, vigils, and education. http:// marchsabbath.org. Download a process of how you can also hold a Gun Violence Prevention Sabbath http://www.nationalcathedral. org/pdfs/SabbathToolkitWNC201303.pdf